PRAISE FOR *JUNGLE RULES*

"Jungle Rules is about business—about tigers and about people. My old friend from Georgia Tech, John Imlay, took a nearly bankrupt company and turned it into a roaring success. He had fun along the way and developed a few rules he now shares with the rest of us.

"John takes us (tracking) through a business jungle full of regulation, litigation, taxes, and takeover artists. Stalked by these predators, he uses tigers for protection and motivation. As we read about the jungle John Imlay conquered, we learn about the perils of business, but, more importantly, we learn about the potential of people. This is a safari you will enjoy."

— SENATOR SAM NUNN

"John has stared the tiger in the eye and beaten the odds. A must read for anyone who puts customers first and has the drive to succeed in a dynamic marketplace."

— HARVEY MACKAY, author of
*Swim with the Sharks Without
Being Eaten Alive*

"Entertainingly instructive. One would be hard put to find a more witty and seasoned guide for surviving and thriving in the business jungle than John Imlay. Entrepreneurs and would-be entrepreneurs will find this book interesting."

— MALCOLM S. FORBES, JR.,
President and Chief Executive Officer,
Editor-in-Chief,
Forbes magazine

"John Imlay's *Jungle Rules* wasn't born out of idle theory, but through scrambling among the grit and perils of the world's toughest business jungles. He presents the rules in the captivating story of a company that was once 24 hours from liquidation and ten years later became the largest company of its kind in the world."

— FRAN TARKENTON,
Chairman, Knowledgeware, Inc.;
NFL Hall of Fame Quarterback

"The title, *Jungle Rules*, captures the imagination, but the content makes you think. This is a 'must-read' book on leadership that will help you master the real world."

—BUCK ROGERS,
author of *The IBM Way*;
International motivational speaker

"Marketing, selling, motivating, imagining, persisting and leading as you never understood it before. Imlay's insights are pure gold. If you've ever wanted to become a tiger in business, *Jungle Rules* will show you how to earn your stripes."

—ROBERT E. WEISSMAN,
President and CEO,
The Dun & Bradstreet Corporation

"For 25 years, John Imlay has been a top speaker in the computer industry. The secret behind his success is anecdotes—vibrant stories that bring lessons to life. I'm happy to report that nothing has been lost in converting his anecdotes to print. *Jungle Rules* is rich in real-life experiences."

—LAWRENCE A. WEINBACH,
Managing Partner—Chief Executive,
Arthur Andersen and Co., SC

"To survive and win as the year 2000 approaches, Imlay goes right to the heart of the matter in *Jungle Rules*. Technology and innovation are only part of the equation. People and human relationships will ultimately determine our success or failure. Congratulations to Imlay for creating a masterful book that brings us back to the basics!"

—STUART R. LEVINE,
CEO,
Dale Carnegie and Associates, Inc.

"Anyone who's built a business will recognize these extraordinary truths. Anyone who's building one will find *Jungle Rules* an incredible roadmap."

—LARRY WELKE,
President,
International Computer Programs, Inc.

JUNGLE RULES

John P. Imlay, Jr.

with Dennis Hamilton

JUNGLE RULES

How to Be a Tiger
in Business

A DUTTON BOOK

DUTTON

Published by the Penguin
Group Penguin Books USA Inc., 375 Hudson Street, New York, New York 10014, U.S.A.
Penguin Books Ltd, 27 Wrights Lane, London W8 5TZ, England
Penguin Books Australia Ltd, Ringwood, Victoria, Australia
Penguin Books Canada Ltd, 10 Alcorn Avenue, Toronto, Ontario, Canada M4V 3B2
Penguin Books (N.Z.) Ltd, 182–190 Wairau Road, Auckland 10, New Zealand

Penguin Books Ltd, Registered Offices:
Harmondsworth, Middlesex, England

First published by Dutton,
an imprint of Dutton Signet,
a division of Penguin Books USA Inc.
Distributed in Canada by McClelland & Stewart Inc.

First Printing, October, 1994
1   3   5   7   9   10   8   6   4   2

REGISTERED TRADEMARK—MARCA REGISTRADA

LIBRARY OF CONGRESS CATALOGING-IN-PUBLICATION DATA:

Imlay, John P.
Jungle rules: how to be a tiger in business / John P. Imlay, Jr.,
with Dennis Hamilton.
p. cm.
Includes index.
ISBN 0-525-93789-7
1. Success in business. 2. Management Science America, Inc.
I. Hamilton, Dennis. II. Title.
HF5386.I463 1994
650.1—dc20   94-8097
CIP

Printed in the United States of America
Set in Gill Sans and Sabon

Designed by Steven N. Stathakis

To the sixteen thousand men and women affiliated with MSA, and subsequently Dun & Bradstreet Software, who gave truth to the idea that people are the key.

CONTENTS

ACKNOWLEDGMENTS   xi

INTRODUCTION: RUN WITH THE TIGERS   I

Part I   THE TIGERS AND THE PHOENIX   7

    I   STALKING THE GOAL   9

    2   SEIZING THE PREY   23

    3   THE FINE ART OF DIRTY WORK   30

    4   MOTIVATING THE TIGERS   4I

    5   NO FLINCHING   59

Part II   RUNNING WITH THE TIGERS   69

    6   TRACKING DOWN THE TIGERS   7I

    7   MANAGING TO LAUGH   8I

8 JUNGLESELLING 90

9 THEM THAT DOES, GETS 106

10 COMPETING IN THE JUNGLE 121

11 RELATIONSHIPS FOR FUN AND PROFIT 133

12 COMMUNICATING IN THE JUNGLE 146

13 LET THE TIGERS RUN 157

14 REMEMBER WHO YOU WORK FOR 164

15 LIONS, TIGERS, AND BEARS 173

Part III EVOLVING WITH THE SPECIES 181

16 PROWLING THE PUBLIC DOMAIN 183

17 THE TIGERS AND THE PEACHTREE 193

18 PREDATORS AT THE DEN 200

19 ANATOMY OF A COMEBACK 210

20 THE COMPROMISES OF EVOLUTION 223

CONCLUSION: IT'S THE PEOPLE 233

INDEX 235

ACKNOWLEDGMENTS

No challenge is more daunting than trying personally to thank everyone who made a business flourish for twenty years—in MSA's case, thousands of people. So I will let the book stand as the symbol of my thanks to them, for it's their story that's told here. But I wanted to express a special gratitude to a few people intimately involved in the writing of the book itself. First, to the sixty people who patiently sat for interviews, who recalled tiger stories that even I had forgotten. To Dennis Hamilton, who took this project not as an assignment but as a labor of love. To Al Zuckerman of The Writer's House, a true literary tiger. To Arnold Dolin of Dutton Signet, who believed in *Jungle Rules* from the first. To Mary Ellen Zubay, my assistant, editor, chastiser, and friend, who patiently read every word of every draft. And to my wife, Geri, and my son, Scott, for traveling the jungle with me, always without complaint.

INTRODUCTION: RUN WITH THE TIGERS

This is a book about a breed of people in business that I call the tigers—the practitioners of the art of stalking success. Not discussing it, not studying it, not waiting for it, not just seeking it, but *stalking* it. And it's a book about the guidelines—the jungle rules— they use to succeed where other business creatures often fail. It's about the adventure of creative thought, the rewards of persistence, the payoff of empowerment, and the exhilaration of doing business in wholly original ways. Welcome to the safari.

Perhaps more than anything, *Jungle Rules* is about finding and developing the tiger in yourself and in the most indispensable element of your success: the people around you.

From the time I first set foot in the business jungle right after college, I began looking for the Immutable Truths—those few timeless laws that will always help businesses succeed. After thirty-six years in business, here are the ones that I've found to be notable.

Businesses succeed through the blunt natural forces of honesty, persistence, and creativity in people—in particular, people who vig-

1

orously pursue their own potential in the context of a team. Everything else is just a vine to swing on.

When I say "jungle," I'm talking about the environment in which businesses must operate. It's an environment that's much at odds with the romantic notions of starting and running businesses in America. Instead of more or less unfettered free enterprise in the land of opportunity, entrepreneurs find something quite different.

They find themselves chopping through thickets of regulations, stalked by litigators, preyed upon by razor-toothed competitors, and drained of blood by leeches from the tax swamp. Neighboring tribes abscond with their best warriors. Yesterday's brilliant product is today's quicksand. And if the jungle can't kill you, it will consume you, putting you on the menu for that beast in the shadows just ahead, the one salivating over a hostile acquisition, a jungle term meaning "dinner."

Is it any wonder that getting through all this was the greatest adventure of my life?

My secret probably goes back to something an old mentor, Mervin Merritt, once told me as a young salesman: "Don't get so smart that you know you're supposed to lose some deals." I guess I never got that smart. Scarcely a day went by in almost two decades with Management Science America, Inc.—the focal company of this safari—that I didn't get excited about a challenge, celebrate a victory, or just laugh out loud. Life's good stuff.

Of course, the jungle is sometimes going to get you down, as it did to us at MSA. What turned out to be important for us was the knowledge that, in the end, it couldn't beat us. We learned we could imagine better, persist longer, fight harder, run faster, and play smarter to overcome all the perils it presented. And we could have fun in the bargain.

In 1971, I took my first proprietary shot at making it through the jungle. A friend and partner, Gene Kelly, and I took over this ailing, near-bankrupt Atlanta company called MSA. It was then an eight-year-old consulting and computer services firm that was millions of dollars in debt and, as far as its creditors were concerned, a prime prospect for bankruptcy liquidation.

Ten years later, it was the largest independent application software company in the world. Nine years after that, in 1990, it was sold to Dun & Bradstreet Corporation for $333 million. It had employed more than sixteen thousand people, generated thirty-eight spinoff companies, and produced twenty millionaires. *Jungle Rules* is about the tigers who made all of that happen.

On one level, it's about how business tigers think, sell, market, motivate, manage, persist, create, envision, and empower in ways that distinguish them from ordinary people.

But *Jungle Rules* is also about the renaissance of the entrepreneur. And how the entrepreneur's aggressive, risk-taking mentality—and intimate knowledge of the marketplace—must return to the boardrooms of big business before the megacorporations end up as an exhibit at the Smithsonian.

On another scale, it's about having fun in the chaos of building and running a business. It's about regaining our seriously eroded people skills in a world that threatens to entomb us in technological cocoons. It's about the role of unconventional management tools—things such as humor, wild animals, and business theater. It's about the dying art of old-fashioned human relationships and how they bind people together in business. It's about maintaining essential civilities in the jungle, such as keeping your word and returning your calls. And it's about finding the light—and sometimes being the light—in the dark times that all businesses and people have.

THE UNCONQUERABLE TIGER

I began devising Jungle Rules because they seemed to apply to a certain breed of people in business that I found myself instinctively attracted to—people who are, in most circumstances, simply unconquerable.

They created, imagined, persisted—they *stalked*—until they achieved their goals. These were people who resisted conventional rules; Jungle Rules allowed them to operate outside of convention. The reasons were simple. Customers are bored by convention, competitors easily counter convention, and employees are unmoved by convention.

They were a motley bunch, these tigers: men and women, with widely differing ethnic backgrounds, and in many sizes and shapes. What they all had in common was a habit of figuring out how to win at business. The most striking thing was that at the heart of their success were their relationships with people.

The guidelines we used are called "Jungle" Rules for three reasons. One was because, having taken over a company in crisis, we made up a lot of new rules just to be able to live through the night—think of it as "survival of the desperate"—when old rules would have put us out of business.

The second was because for twenty years we used exotic animals as our corporate themes, live and in person at company functions, and throughout our literature. That's how I acquired the reputation as the man who brings Bengal tigers to parties.

The third reason is because the jungle, by its nature, emphasizes the individual, the lone creature. No gadgetry, no fads, no electronic crutches.

Perhaps the most important thing to know is that Jungle Rules do exactly the opposite of what most rules do—that is, confine you, constrict you, even oppress you. Jungle Rules liberate you. They free you to think, to act, to imagine. Jungle Rules define what people can do, not what they cannot.

And people are what this book is about.

There is an old maxim about buying real estate. Success depends on three things: location, location, and location. Similarly, business success depends on people, people, and people.

The right people will give you products, markets, resourcefulness, imagination, organization, and execution—all the ingredients for success. Unfortunately, we've devoted much of the last half century to nonhuman aspects—all important, but all secondary. Now, as we head into the year 2000, there has never been a greater need to reexamine ourselves, our people, our relationships, and our business conduct more critically.

A GENERATION TRAPPED IN THE TECHNOLOGY COCOON

You've seen them. You might even be one. Eight hours every shift, day after day, staring at the computer screen, sending memos down the line, scanning graphics on the terminal, massaging information in the databases, leaving digitized messages. Receding little by little from humanity. You suspect they are alive, but still . . .

Thanks to today's technology, we can—that is, some *think* we can—conduct business in utter isolation. And many business people have been conditioned to think that's just fine, which is not surprising, considering that our educational system today has about a 20:1 ratio of technology classes to interpersonal skills training.

Thanks to constellations of computer networks, knowledge bases, robotics, executive information systems, and decision support systems, we can, if we choose, try to run our businesses without ever crossing the path of another living organism.

People now can be hired, fired, promoted, and demoted via voice mail. Bo Schembechler, when he was president of the Detroit Tigers, was pink-slipped over a fax machine. Holiday wishes are sincerely expressed by automatic handwriting devices. Selling is being conducted by automated calling. "Personal" messages are sent by electronic mail. Company meetings are held by teleconference. Quality control is measured in machine tolerances instead of client satisfaction. Customers have stopped being people and become database files. Little by little, human beings have grown dependent upon daily fixes of techno-crack.

One result is a business world in which people relate less and less to one another as human beings. Instead, we have all become someone's abstractions—a file number, a key word, a module on a network. Our high-tech systems, procedures, and shortcuts have left us masters of everything but the endangered art of human interaction—the first, most constant, and most important art in business.

What's ahead? Will we still be able to converse with a face that isn't digitized on a screen? Will we really empathize with the needs of an encoded mailing label? Will we be able to "sense" a new market with a four-color pie chart?

What we now have is a generation of business people who tend to go down when their systems go down. They have lost the ability to think on their feet, to take personal command of a situation, to imagine ideas and dimensions beyond those suggested by the menus on their personal computer screens.

You might ask: Who is this guy laying waste to our fixation with technology? I say all of this as Chairman of Dun & Bradstreet Software Services, Inc.—at $550 million, one of the largest software technology companies in the world. The truth is, I love technology. I think the software industry might be the most important industry on earth for its ability to streamline business and manufacturing, improve the quality of decisions, and boost human productivity. Better than most, I appreciate its utterly vital role in our personal lives and our collective success. But I'm also in an unusual position to see how it has distracted us from thinking about people.

If there is one transcendent Jungle Rule in our high-tech world, it is this: *People are the key.* And I have always tried to keep my focus on people and the relationships that empower them to succeed.

Jungle Rules is about finding, teaching, mobilizing, and motivating the tiger in business people and then turning them loose to succeed. What all of us at MSA learned about people and management and leadership transcends our story about a computer software company that once was twenty-four hours from liquidation and came to lead the world in one of its most important technologies. It's about the kinds of people who will lead many of the businesses of tomorrow.

And this book shows how, when the jungle is at its darkest and most forbidding, when you sense a predator nearby, when all seems lost, the game is just beginning.

Part I

*The phoenix is a legendary bird,
which, by at least one account, lived
500 years, burned itself to ashes
on a pyre, and rose youthfully
alive from the ashes to live again.
The phoenix became the first animal,
mythical or otherwise, to
symbolize the business
adventures of a company in ashes
that rose to become the largest
enterprise of its kind in the
world. But it was the tigers—the
people who took that company
through the business jungle—who
made the rebirth possible. Told
in the rules by which they played
the game, this is their story.*

I

STALKING THE GOAL

Jungle Rule #1:
Believe in fate, but stalk your goal.

I begin with goals because almost everything important begins with goals. Most of us have talked about goal setting since childhood, but there is uncomfortable evidence that we never made goal setting a goal. Even fewer of us have made goal stalking a practice. We rely too much on fate. We talk, we dream, we admire, we covet. But do we accomplish? Are we really good at goals or just going through the motions? It's easy to find out: How many of your goals have you achieved? If the honest answer is "Not many," you might be letting life happen instead of making it happen.

Fairly early in life, I came up with my first important goal: I wanted to own a business in Atlanta. That might seem general and simple, as goals go. It's not. A lot of goal-setting advocates suggest excruciatingly specific goals, but I think it's important to have latitude enough to maneuver, to improvise. Stalking is seldom done in a straight line. It's a process of circling, closing in, then at precisely the right moment, attacking.

Business persons often thwart their goals with too many

straight-line, chisled-in-granite specifics—"I want to make at least $65,000 and become assistant vice president of circulation by next year, have a dozen people reporting to me, a company car, stock options, a health club membership, a private window office with a good view, and bonus-plan eligibility." And so forth. The problem is, fail anywhere and you consider that you've failed, period. The thing to do is to figure out what's really important, then stalk that.

In truth, specifics are for tactics and operations. Goals are the inspiration. If you can't state your goal in a simple sentence—"I want to sing at the Met" or "I want to be a pro golfer" or "I want to be teacher of the year"—it's too complicated. Once you make the judgment, then stick with it. Let the stalking begin.

There are many penalties for failing to set and stalk goals. The most painful to me is that, if you don't set your goal, someone else will set it for you, perhaps for your entire life. It won't have anything to do with your aspirations, but it will have everything to do with theirs. And while sharing goals is fine—even necessary, as we'll discuss—the process should be a two-way street. You help them through the jungle and they help you. But before anyone can help you get somewhere, you have to know where you're going. It's as simple as that.

And fate? There's no doubt that fate has something in store for you, as it does for us all. But whether it is your goal is highly questionable. Fate, after all, is inevitable; your goal is not.

Set the goal, then stalk the goal. You can't end up a winner in a world where you haven't decided what to conquer.

GOAL SHARING: BE AN ALLY, FIND AN ALLY

Sometimes the best way to gain an ally for your own goals is to become an ally for someone else's. One way is through a wonderful process called goal sharing.

Eddie Robinson is the legendary football coach at Grambling State University near Rushton, Louisiana, where he still is coaching after more than fifty years. Robinson is an instinctive goal sharer. In his first season at Grambling in 1941, the father of his two star running backs urgently ordered his sons home because he needed their help to pick his crops.

Robinson recognized the father's goal—survival—so he decided to share in it. He loaded up the entire Grambling team, took them to the farm, and had them pick the fields clean. The father let the brothers return, and Grambling went on to win the league championship.

Great relationships—and subsequently games, careers, and companies—are built on helping other people achieve their goals. These are people who eventually reciprocate by helping you achieve yours. It's nice when you can accomplish yours in tandem with theirs. The key is not to make your own goals secondary forever.

The secret is control, a sometimes scary word. As used here, it absolutely does not mean being dictatorial. Dictatorships fail miserably in business just as they do in politics. Anyone who thinks that Mussolini just had a misunderstood management style that would translate well to business will end up hanging—figuratively, of course—from the corporate flagpole. The notion of a democracy of ideas is vital not only for cultivating strong relationships, but for building better companies through competitive thinking.

Control is different. Once the goal is in place, control means simply having the *information* to make good decisions and the *autonomy* to act on them.

To have control, then, you don't have to own your own company. While many business tigers do eventually end up with their own companies because they are aggressive and high-goal oriented, others are content to use Jungle Rules just to do their jobs better.

Control, as we define it, can be found (or not found) in any job, including chief executive. It can take the form of what is called intrapreneurship—internal entrepreneurship—where an individual literally starts and runs a kind of informal subsidiary within a company; project leadership, in which a great deal of autonomy is granted; field sales, where the salesperson is given the freedom to make spontaneous, creative, independent decisions that might not be found in even the most liberal employee handbook; and even, as we will shortly demonstrate, greeting customers, at least when the job is perceived to be more than cheerful hellos.

A tiger doesn't have to own a company, but he has to own something, and *information* and *autonomy* are at the top of the list. Jungle advisory: Any goal is doomed without the freedom to succeed.

GOALS BELONG TO ANYONE WHO SETS THEM

People who are good at goal setting and control run the gamut of personalities. You know some of the great ones. The late Sam Walton of the Wal-Mart empire built his business on this simple rule: "By cutting your price, you can boost your sales to a point where you can earn far more at the cheaper retail price than by selling the item at the higher price." That's a billion-dollar thought. His idea was that simple, and, in 1962 (when the first Wal-Mart store opened and the discount boom got hot), he was that visionary. Walton himself was folksy, reclusive, and modest.

Ross Perot, late of Electronic Data Systems and iconoclastic presidential campaigns, is, conversely, complex, high profile, and stern. Lee Iacocca, now retired from Chrysler Corporation, is attention loving, image conscious, and charismatic. Three obviously different men, but all goal oriented, all successful.

The universe of business tigers is varied in that they arrive with every imaginable profile. But there are relatively few to be found. What they all illustrate is that goal setting should be a personality trait and not just a business exercise—and that goals can help everyone from the CEO to the receptionist.

Cases in point.

One of my favorite goal setters is Fran Tarkenton, the NFL Hall of Fame quarterback who played for the Minnesota Vikings and the New York Giants. Tarkenton has been a good friend and golfing nemesis since 1971, and—it will surprise most people—is today one of the leading executives in the computer software industry.

Whatever he undertakes, in sports, business, or life, his first act is setting a goal. As a star athlete at the University of Georgia, he decided his first career goal was to be a quarterback in professional football. It wasn't to play for the Minnesota Vikings or the New York Giants or to get to the Hall of Fame or to set a dozen passing and scoring records in the NFL. It was to get to a point where subsequent goals would be possible.

As Bob Knight, the Hall of Fame basketball coach for Indiana University, said when talking about the goal of a game, "You want to be in position to be in position." That is, keep yourself in the game, then be in the best position possible to win in the end: stalk until you can strike.

When Tarkenton played football, he was a lightning-quick opportunist. His goal on the field was to score. It was elegantly simple. He would use pre-game tactics—60:40 pass-to-run ratios and so forth—but his great skill was that he could scramble if the tactics weren't working. Tigers don't freeze up even when the wheels come off a plan. Tarkenton could improvise. He could stalk. He could *do what was necessary*. He had cultivated those assets that put him in control of his goal.

In 1971, when I first contacted him about becoming a spokesman for Management Science America (a relationship that lasted several years), I had to explain to him what software was (he thought it was sweaters). But his post-NFL goal was to develop himself as a businessman and start his own enterprises.

Ten years later, his playing days over, he was looking at acquiring a small company. By chance, the company—it was called Knowledgeware—had a software product called a code generator, which is a tool used to do computer programming more automatically than old manual techniques. At that point, he knew enough about the software world—"We had to find better ways to build applications," he said—to make a quick and comfortable decision. First goal achieved. Next goal: make the company a leader.

"My goals are simple," he says. "If my products make my customers better off, they'll buy them. If my products don't, they won't. If my earnings are good, people will buy my stock. If they're not, they will sell my stock. So everything I do is focused on those two goals."

But you don't have to be an NFL Hall of Famer to be a business tiger. Consider Twila Lowe.

Twila's job was to greet visitors at MSA and run the switchboard—but she did it with the tireless care of someone who had a stake in every call and every greeting (a common attitude among these people). She had this wonderful, honey-sweet Georgia accent that could win over any caller. It never wavered even when talking to clients in MSA's darkest days, when money was out, morale had gone south, the press was head-hunting, creditors were screaming, and people were losing their jobs all around her. Hers was the first voice callers heard and the first face visitors saw.

As a tiger, Twila never looked upon her job as a "receptionist" or a "switchboard operator." Her job, as she defined it, was *first impressions* and *problem solving*. Her calm in the eye of the storm saved a lot of clients.

Her subsequent goal was related, but loftier (as subsequent goals should be). And the way to it had been paved by her experience as a receptionist (she was "in position to be in position"). A few years after I took over, she asked if she could move into marketing—a difficult business because it involved selling mainframe-level computer software to sophisticated technicians and high-level financial people in large companies. I saw her potential and gave her the chance.

She learned the nuances of the marketplace and the MSA style of marketing. Then she turned an understanding of the company's resources and inner workings she had cultivated at the switchboard into problem-solving customer support. Her first year out, she won MSA's Rookie of the Year Award in a field loaded with talent.

Whatever the position you hold, from CEO to receptionist, the key to success is having the freedom to think—and act—on your feet so that you can gain and maintain control of your goal. The second is being able to truly understand your job beyond its conventional description, as both Fran Tarkenton and Twila Lowe do. Are you a salesman or a *problem solver?* Anyone can ask for the business, but far fewer are willing to solve tough problems to get it. Are you a manager or a *leader?* A manager can write reports and watch numbers, but far fewer can lead people through the jungle. A quarterback or a *winner?* There have been lots of quarterbacks; far fewer have been winners.

And then there is your environment. The reason business tigers do not flourish in some companies is not because too many people lack initiative and imagination. There's plenty of that if someone just frees it, but some firms discourage initiative and imagination— and forbid autonomy—while rewarding timid adherence to old rules that constrict people. These environments are like elephants' graveyards, where even the most magnificent goals go to die. And potential tigers die right along with them, declawed and infertile.

As someone once said, only dead fish swim with the stream.

BEWARE THE GOAL BEYOND YOUR CONTROL

Here's a cautionary tale for goal stalkers.

MSA started fast, grew phenomenally, then crashed precipitously because no one was stalking its goal. And after a while, it just ceased to have one.

MSA was begun with the simplest of goals—"just completing projects well," as cofounder Bill Graves put it. But there was palpable energy and imagination from the outset, and those are indispensable ingredients in the stalking of any goals.

The company was founded in the spring of 1963 by five graduates of Georgia Tech, headed by Dr. Tom Newberry, a sharp doctoral graduate whose Ph.D. was in industrial engineering.

Starting with seven employees in 1963, MSA had grown nicely—and profitably—to one hundred employees by 1967, most of them consultants to the textile industry. That year it showed a modest profit of $60,000 on revenue of $981,000. But that profit was good enough to land the company a private stock placement and two multimillion-dollar loans—a total of about $8 million—to begin expanding into what seemed at the time to be an infinite market. "We felt invulnerable," said Jim Edenfield, another bright, young Georgia Tech graduate who joined MSA's management team shortly after its incorporation. "Everything we touched turned to gold."

That's when goals usually depart from reality.

It was in 1968 that I had my first of three terms of employment with MSA. I had been working as a salesman with a fellow named Russ Henderson at Honeywell at the time. That year, I had sold MSA twenty Honeywell computers for a new venture that was underway. They liked my selling style well enough to offer me a job as vice president of marketing. The idea of joining a small but growing enterprise interested me, so I accepted.

The company was expanding out of consulting and was opening computer centers—service bureaus—in major cities across the country and in London. They were so confident in the market that they built the computer centers with no revenue. They just bought the computers, plugged them in, hired full staffs and sales forces, and hit the street with celestial expectations.

And there was more. Besides the computer centers, there was a travel agency, an interior decorating firm, a healthcare systems company, a personnel agency, an advertising agency, and an entirely new kind of business called software products. As I watched that year, MSA boosted its ranks of consultants at the rate of fifty per month, growing from fifty-five to 350, all with vice president titles. I could see that this was going to be a spectacular success or a cataclysmic failure, and it wasn't long before I began leaning toward the latter.

If MSA came tumbling down, the crash was going to bury a lot of people. In the private stock placement, several of the officials of First National Bank bet their own money on the MSA venture in addition to granting the company a bank loan of $3 million. While this wasn't technically illegal, it represented a conflict of interest. If things should go sour, the bank officers would be faced with the choice of losing their own money in a failure or investing even more of the bank's money in the hopes of turning MSA around and recouping their personal investments.

With Bill Graves's original goal long gone, replaced by a vision of some kind of multiheaded holding company, the situation continued to decline. I was fired after seven months for objecting to the out-of-control spending. But shortly thereafter, Tom Newberry and Jim Edenfield were canned by the bank (which now held their stock) for failing to turn things around. By 1969, the company's losses had reached an astronomical $5,109,000.

MSA's leaders had stopped stalking the goal they had set. Now the business had turned them into the prey.

WHEN YOU GET CONTROL, DON'T LOSE CONTROL

One of the dangers of autonomy—whether you own the company or just have great freedom in your position—is excess. It's the "Toos Disease"—too much, too many, too big, too fast, too soon, and so on. Tigers in business are imaginative and adventurous, but they usually are not incautious.

MSA, like many other companies of the day, suffered from incautious excess. Easy money was available. Decisions were unchallenged. The world was their oyster. No one foresaw the recession. The people in control had lost control. Inevitably, when you lose control, you end up being controlled, and your destiny is no longer yours to determine. Most of the founders and principals were out of the business, debt was astronomical and rising, and a sense of desperation was setting in.

Yet all that was needed to begin the correction was a simple sentence—stating a new goal.

It's a common problem in business. Crisis often has a domino effect, especially when units of a company are interdependent. When one goes, they all are in danger. Then the problems become magnified again. There is not *a* personnel problem, there are several personnel problems, one in each unit. Every unit has cash flow difficulties. Every unit has declining morale. Every unit has creditors screaming.

And every unit has a different goal, and each is out of control.

It all becomes a blue haze of accusation and blame and eventually defections and failure—unless, that is, a fresh eye can cut through the haze to find the new goal.

When you sense that a goal has been lost or is out of control —or is just wrong—it's imperative to cut through that haze. Sometimes it can be done internally, but all sorts of factors (company politics, subjective loyalties, etc.) work against that. Often only a fresh outside eye, one uncontaminated by the company's history, can see the truth. Either way, you've got to regain control of the goal before you can make any other decisions. And you don't have long to do it.

The Toos Disease has struck every business at some time or another. It can hit a company like an act of God. Too many business interests, too little revenue, too big a debt, too many sacred cows (one of the business jungle's most feared predators).

Pulled in a dozen directions by old priorities, competing interests, and to some extent ego ("I *know* we can make this old goal work!"), management will be consumed by the Toos Disease until fresh eyes are brought in to look things over and try to regain lost control.

I'm often stunned at how crisis managers and even boards of directors get a bad rap because they are "outsiders." But that's why their view is invaluable. Whatever your business, you should have fresh eyes look it over with some regularity. Emotional conviction is fine—is cherished—when things are sailing along, but dispassion provides a better view of the race.

CRISIS IS THE BEST PLACE TO START A NEW BUSINESS

The great thing about a crisis is that there is little downward mobility. The only real direction to go is up. Crisis managers have no allegiances to sacred cows. They don't know or care about the old office politics. They have great clarity in their fresh eyes. And the whole electric experience of dancing through minefields conditions your reflexes for crises to come. Every aspiring executive should do a stint in crisis management.

I draw a distinction between crisis managers and consultants. The latter come in, observe, pass notes to someone in authority, and mail an invoice. Crisis managers are different beasts. For one, they are *empowered* to change things. For another, they fail if those changes don't work. There is a lot more on the line for crisis managers, and that's why it's the better training ground for business tigers.

After being fired by MSA, I sat down with a close friend, an ex-FBI accountant named Gene Kelly, and we began making plans to stalk our goals by starting a facilities management business in Atlanta. Facilities management—FM, as it's known—is where computer specialists come into a business's computer installation and run it, usually more profitably and efficiently than the business was able to do.

Before we could get started, we were invited by another old friend, E. W. "Mac" McCain, to come to work for him as crisis managers—going into troubled companies and trying to sort out problems, products, politics, and priorities. It turned out to be the most important conditioning I could have had to prepare me for my own business.

Kelly was Mr. Inside, the analyst, the peruser of the books. I was Mr. Outside, the voice, the salesman, the executor of the scripts. It would prove to be a good combination.

Maurice "Ted" Maloof, longtime attorney for MSA:

John and Gene had a reputation for being able to turn companies around. John was the motivator and Gene was

19

the investigator. John was this brilliant marketer. Gene was his archangel. Gene could look at details and get right down to the nitty-gritty of any problem. Then he'd give them to John and say, "See ya."

One of our crisis challenges was a company that looked a lot like MSA. The firm was an eighteen-month-old Jacksonville, Florida, business called Computer Technology/South. It was a candidate to become a subsidiary of University Computing Company, the firm that had hired Kelly and me as crisis managers.

But CT/South had been having profitability problems. Before UCC chairman Sam Wyly would buy it, he wanted to see whether it was salvageable.

We found that it was a disaster. It was such a disaster, with so many conspicuous problems, that we couldn't understand why action hadn't been taken before our arrival. But as we came to learn, that paralysis is common to a company in crisis. Should we abandon our goals? Are we giving up too quickly? Do we need (yet another) tactical plan to turn things around? If I can't make this company work, will I be a failure?

But if you walk clean into a crisis, none of that affects you.

When CT/South was formed, the company had hired about one hundred top-level IBM executives with five-year, very expensive contracts. The object was to roar out of the gates with lots of tenure and knowledge. It had done this, like MSA, with little revenue, and the cost was eating the company alive.

And there were other problems. Like MSA, interior decoration was from the school of excess. The company had spent literally millions of dollars on furnishings, including such commonsense necessities as leopard skin rugs. The first day in the offices we kept hearing the phone ringing, but couldn't find the phone. It turned out to be inside a hand-carved box that every executive had on his desk. We figured there had to be a vice president of excess around there somewhere.

It was evident what needed to be done. A massive restructuring was necessary to salvage the company. Without the baggage of old goals, old politics, old privileges—and old leopard skin rugs—we could see clearly through the blue haze. The good news was that in the middle of it, there was a viable business, begging to be extricated. It was here we began to get a sense that crisis is the best place to start a new business.

Why crisis? For one thing, presumably, a real business had existed here before its goals became muddled and sank it. It was a matter of finding it, scraping off the barnacles, and sending it to the surface. For another, there are resources in place: people, procedures, products. Reorganizing them, redirecting them, and redeploying them can be much simpler than starting from scratch. Third, there are customers. True, some of them might be completely alienated, but chances are many others are salvageable.

Crises inherently have a tremendous amount of energy. Much of it is like the flailing of the drowning swimmer, but that adrenalin can be put to good use if you turn the flailing into swimming strokes. That, of course, is called leadership.

This is what we did.

JUNGLE RULE SUMMARY

BELIEVE IN FATE, BUT STALK YOUR GOAL.

Set your goal, then do something every day to make it happen.

GOAL SHARING: BE AN ALLY, FIND AN ALLY

Learn and practice the art of goal sharing.

GOALS BELONG TO ANYONE WHO SETS THEM

Goal setting is your birthright, so don't forsake it; but goal achievement is strictly up to you.

JUNGLE RULES

BEWARE THE GOAL BEYOND YOUR CONTROL

Once you have a goal in mind, don't let it get out of hand.

WHEN YOU GET CONTROL, DON'T LOSE CONTROL

Once you have a goal in hand, don't let it get out of mind.

CRISIS IS THE BEST PLACE TO START A NEW BUSINESS

There's a pony in there somewhere.

2

SEIZING THE PREY

Jungle Rule #2:
Lay out your plan, then strike like a cat.

One great lesson of crisis management is that patience is no virtue.

Once you know what you have to do, you do it. When the plan is in place, the sudden strike is the only way to execute it. The old passions, politics, and priorities are like Velcro: They'll stick to you if your pace is too slow.

The biggest impediments to restructuring CT/South were the five-year contracts with the ex-IBMers. They all marched in to me, wingtips shining, and defiantly said I could not fire them, which technically was true.

"I can't fire you," I replied, "but I can transfer you to Waco, Texas. We can't pay your moving expenses, and you'll be working for the meanest guy in Waco for the rest of your contract."

They lined up, took minimal severance pay, and left that day.

A harsh rule of the jungle? Not really. It was not a matter of being cold or unfair, just realistic. Without swift action, the company would die and the squadron of IBMers would have been out on the street anyway. And there was no use prolonging what we knew to be inevitable. Once a decision is made, you act. You do not falter. If you can, you carry it out in days rather than weeks, hours rather than days, minutes rather than hours.

Before Kelly and I left CT/South, we'd reduced staff by 50 percent, closed the most opulent offices, auctioned off the rugs and baubles, and even sold some long-term contracts. It was all perfect experience for our next job—MSA.

In terms of our goals, Kelly and I were about to find out, as Bob Knight puts it, that we had put ourselves "in position to be in position."

Bill Matthews, the new president of First National Bank of Atlanta, called UCC chairman Sam Wyly and said he needed Kelly and me right away to take a shot at salvaging MSA. Wyly agreed and the bank "rented" the two of us for $8,000 a month. We went in with our fresh eyes and started poring over the numbers, talking to people, and getting a feel for the true depth of the financial, organizational, and morale problems.

By week's end, we had again seen through the haze. And like CT/South, there was a business lying hidden within MSA. We presented the only solution we could reasonably arrive at: All of the consulting had to go; all of the computer centers had to be shut down; all of the unrelated businesses—the interior decorator, travel agency, personnel agency—had to be disbanded.

There was a solitary business remaining that we thought had a shot at becoming profitable: the small software products venture.

In 1971, software products constituted a relatively new idea. The premise was simple: It made vastly more sense to write a computer program once, copy it for a few dollars (literally), then sell the copies to a large, essentially common client base rather than to laboriously—and expensively—reinvent the wheel with every customer.

The future, of course, would prove this idea to be as revolutionary as Sam Walton's notion about discounting.

We calculated that it would cost one-tenth as much to buy software as it would to develop the same thing in-house. And it would be up and running in one-tenth of the time. The economics all around were stunning to contemplate. But in those early days, it wasn't an easy sell.

Software products, despite the seemingly radiant common sense of the idea, hadn't yet caught on with the public. Programmers, who had great influence in the decisions about buying, resented them because they thought products could put them out of a job; and IBM had been giving away its software whenever it sold a computer, so there had been little incentive for companies to lay out money for products.

Don House, former vice president of marketing, MSA:

What we did trying to sell software back then was almost evangelical. You would search for someone who had even half an understanding of what you are talking about. When you found them, they were usually adversarial—the data processing managers who were afraid of losing their jobs to this new idea. But at least they could understand. We somehow had to make the concept of software products understandable to more people. We likened it to a player piano, which is run off of a punched tape. Slowly people began to get it.

A couple of things happened at this time that gave this new concept some hope. After pressure from the U.S. Department of Justice over monopolistic practices, IBM on January 1, 1970, had begun charging separately for its application software (the software that performs business tasks such as accounting or word processing). And since companies now had to pay, they might start giving independent software companies a closer look. This was because most of the free software products from IBM were the technical equivalent of hot-air balloons in the jet age.

This was the opening MSA needed to succeed.

We presented the plan to the bank. After describing the commercial idea behind software products—something few people contemplated in early 1971—we told them that MSA already had a significant asset in its 350 blue-chip customers. There was also a tax-loss carryforward of up to $16 million.

"I recommend you buy the company," I told them. "The software products can be highly profitable, and you would not pay taxes. But everything else has to go."

The bank officers looked at Kelly and me. "Do you want this challenge?" they asked, meaning: Were we interested in managing MSA back to profitability? These were bankers, not entrepreneurs. Their chief concern—their goal—was retrieving the money they'd put into the venture before worse came to worst. While they had a primitive understanding of the software business from our explanation, they weren't inclined to go into the business, whatever its potential.

Neither, at first, were Kelly and I. There was fierce pressure coming from creditors who were about to garnish payroll checks. Rent hadn't been paid in certain places. If we were to take the job, we said, we would need to file bankruptcy so that we could do the reorganization without interference.

And, oh yes—we wanted to own the company when we got through.

Gene Kelly:

We had these little jobs coming up all the time because of word of mouth about what we were doing turning around these companies. We'd work on these companies that had financial problems. It began to dawn on us that we'd lost our original goal. We were going to own the company. We were going to be making some money. We were killing ourselves making a lot of money for someone else, but it wasn't finding its way into our pockets. So we said, next time we get a chance, before we go into any deal, we're going to say we want a chance to buy the damn company.

We had prepared, we had stalked, and now we had recognized opportunity. The next step was to spring at it.

SEIZE THE DAY

There is an old story about seizing opportunity. This religious fellow once got caught in a rainstorm that turned into a flood. He climbed up on his roof as the flood waters rose. After a while, a man in a rowboat paddled up. "Jump in," the rower said. "No," the roof sitter replied. "God will watch over me." The waters rose. Now they were at the roofline. Another rowboat arrived. "Jump in!" the rower told him. "No," the man said again. "God will watch over me." The waters rose higher. They were at his feet. A helicopter suddenly descended from above and dropped a rope. "Grab hold," the pilot said, "I'll pull you up." The man said, "No, God will watch over me." Shortly afterward, the flood washed over the roof, and the man was swept away and drowned. When he got to heaven, he confronted God and demanded to know why He hadn't saved him. Replied God, "I sent two boats and a helicopter, what *more* do you want?!"

The Latin phrase is *carpe diem*—seize the day. It is one of the most vital rules of business and life. If you subscribe to the theory that life comes down to a few moments—and the decisions you make in those moments shape what happens to you—then you know the value of being ready to seize the day.

Kelly and I understood two situations well. One was our own. We wanted to start a business in Atlanta, we had no real capital to do it with, and we knew the computer industry. The other situation was the bank's. The bank had control of a business it didn't want. And the investors needed someone to clean it up and get them off the hook for the loans. The question was whether they would be willing to part with control of the company.

"What do you propose?" they asked.

We wanted control.

"We want ten percent of the company if you sell it," I said. I literally was making up the arrangement on the spur of the moment. All of the tumblers had clicked into place to open this door. "If we get you your money back, we get your stock."

27

Everyone traded glances with everyone else, then Ed Smith, the bank chairman, stood and extended his hand. "Done," he said.

Gene Kelly:

Imlay and I are walking back after we did the deal. Neither of us has enough money to hire a cab. We walked six blocks to Peachtree Center. On the walk back, I got tickled and started laughing. He asked, "What in the hell are you laughing about?" I said, "Boy, we're really big financiers. Here are two country boys, one from Savannah and one from Monticello. Twenty minutes ago, we were honest, free Americans and didn't owe anybody a penny. Now you and I are slaves to a company that is twelve million dollars in debt." He said, "You know, I never really thought about it that way." It suddenly dawned on us that while we didn't have enough money for a cab ride, we did have enough for two Miller beers. We went into this little bar and took our last eighty cents to congratulate each other on going twelve million dollars in debt.

The key to prospering in these situations is recognition. Kelly and I had three assets that made our move viable: one, we wanted to be in business; two, having looked at the MSA books, we thought the software business could fly with a new, focused goal in place; and three, we knew the secured creditors were approaching desperation.

Recognition, and the willingness to act fairly boldly on our feet, had given us a rare opportunity: to acquire a company with no cash and no collateral. Now all we had to do was execute a plan that would deliver what we promised. And make sure that, having gotten control, we didn't lose it.

We began with a new goal for MSA: *We would be a profitable software services company with a personal touch.* Simple sentence. Not so simple problem.

And Tom Newberry and Jim Edenfield? In the end, they proved

unconquerable. At MSA they lost control and it cost them. But the two of them within weeks cofounded another software company, American Software, Inc., in Atlanta. They never lost control again, growing it into a powerhouse provider of software for large- and medium-sized computers.

Above all, tigers in business never stop learning.

JUNGLE RULE SUMMARY

LAY OUT YOUR PLAN, THEN STRIKE LIKE A CAT.

Don't procrastinate. Don't act without a plan, but don't hesitate with one.

SEIZE THE DAY

If you have stalked your goal, it will eventually cross your path. Take it instantly or risk losing it.

3

THE FINE ART OF DIRTY WORK

Jungle Rule #3:
A fight to the last person has no winner.

I was going through an airport one evening, and I saw John coming out. He looked so bad, so tired. He couldn't even speak. I later learned this was about the time he had fired four hundred people.

—A. P. "PETE" JENSEN,
Georgia Tech University

There are two reasons why I started this book dealing with crisis. One is that I spent my first year at MSA hopping from the frying pan to the fire and back, so it is chronologically correct. More important, anyone who seeks control will automatically inherit crisis, so it's important to know how to deal with it.

Bill Botts, an ex-astronaut hired to lead MSA the year before, was ousted as president on February 26, 1971, when I was appointed general manager. He felt he had been wronged and along with a band of key employees met to discuss starting their own software company to compete with MSA. The résumés of many of our employees began to fill the air like locusts. Never had Atlanta's technology community had such an explosion of applicants.

The plan for saving MSA was brutally clear. Of the existing organization, all of the eighteen U.S. computer centers would have to be closed down, along with the center in London. Virtually all of the consultants would have to be dismissed. The personnel agency, advertising agency, interior decorator, travel agency, and healthcare systems company all had to be dissolved. All told, about 740 people had to be severed from MSA. Only fifty-seven people from the software products section and administration would remain.

The applicable Jungle Rule here—"A fight to the last person has no winner"—is simple, more valiant than it sounds, and excruciatingly true. There was considerable pressure on us to keep the organization intact and reorganize in a less brutal way. But our analysis told us that would be like rearranging deck chairs on the *Titanic*. If we battled to the last person, we might have been remembered as valiant fools, but fools nonetheless. In business, the only thing the "last person" does, once the smoke clears, is get subpoenaed to court to distribute the assets.

While Kelly and I fully recognized that 740 living, breathing human beings were on the line here, we had to focus on the fifty-seven people who were staying. It wasn't easy. Bill Matthews of First National Bank, for one, told me the cuts were too drastic and not to make them.

I made them anyway.

I had the two things I needed in this relationship with the bank—*autonomy* and *information*—so I had confidence in my decision and the authority to carry it out. We had agreed to share the bank's goal of regaining its investment, and the bank had agreed to share our goal of acquiring the company once it was done. But the necessary ingredient of control came with our autonomy. This prevented us from being undermined by old sensitivities, creeping politics, and second thoughts. That safeguard turned out to be key to our success.

The truth is, few people want to do dirty work, and a lot of people like to undermine it. Autonomy is your shield against all of them—including being forced into a no-win battle to the last person.

DIRTY WORK IS BEST DONE CLEANLY

This means you don't wrestle yourself two out of three falls over every decision. It's like the guy who was walking along with his chronically ambivalent friend. "Do you have trouble making up your mind?" he asked. Replied his friend, "Well, yes and no."

Sometimes the dirtier the work is, the more we have a tendency to second-guess ourselves. We look to mitigate the seeming harshness of our decisions, to hope for a white knight or an inheritance or greater wisdom. In truth, your first analysis is usually the best. Dragging things out is just that.

I gave myself three days to do what needed to be done.

I asked Gene Kelly to give me lists of all of the employees who would be dismissed in our plan. I then flew from city to city requesting that employees meet me at the airports. There I delivered their termination notices en masse and answered their questions as well as I could.

In some instances, I located the supervisors and managers, then had them notify the employees that they had been terminated in the reorganization. When the managers reported back to me, I would dismiss them. Once, after going to a site to inform the employees they were being given pink slips, I asked the manager to drive me back to the airport, where I then told him we could not keep him in the reorganization. For years afterward, people looked mock-horrified (maybe it wasn't mock) when I asked them to drive me to an airport.

Gene Kelly:

We moved so quickly. People were still bringing customers and prospects in and making presentations to them. They would bring the customers in to meet the president, which

*was customary. Then John would close the sale and termi-
nate the salesman. It got confusing as hell. John would
lose track of what he was doing. He fired George Grimes,
our man in England. George wanted money to come
home. John said, "I'm sorry, there is no money. We're
bankrupt." Later, we found the money to get him home.
Then he fired Bill Graves over the phone in New Jersey.
He told John, "You can't fire me. I'm the only one who
knows what's going on." John says, "Well, you're terminated." Graves says, "Let me come down and tell you
why you can't fire me." John says, "Okay." Graves convinced him. By now it was chaos. People were going out
back ways, stealing tapes, closing down complete departments. That was all on a Friday. We filed bankruptcy on
the following Monday, after all the dirty work had been
done.*

During one frenzied meeting at MSA's Atlanta headquarters, during which we closed all of the subsidiary businesses and fired most of the personnel not affiliated with the software products operation, I passed out pink slips to about fifteen people in the room. There was one man in the room, a fellow named Jerry MacElhattan, who adamantly kept insisting that I could not fire him.

"I'm sorry," I told him as I made my way back to my office. "But we have no choice. This company is going under if we don't do this."

"You can't fire me," he said, following me into the office. "I don't work for you. I'm the controller for the Cleveland Bank and Trust Company."

I had just fired a prospective customer.

Fortunately, he let me explain what I was doing and why, instead of just storming out. When I was done, he told me he understood the strategy. Before he left, he signed the contract.

He and Bill Graves were about the only people who survived our single-minded ax that week. Naturally, I was glad to keep a customer. I wasn't so sure about Graves until he made his pitch to me and convinced me that he believed in the future of the software industry and had more knowledge about MSA's software products than anyone else.

Pete Jensen:

John found value in Bill Graves, who was a very key component. Bill was the technical brains of what evolved at MSA. Fundamentally, he was the fellow who made things go, the guy who was the architect of all the software that came out. Contrary to all of us technocrats who said that IBM technology was not what it ought to be, he said that it was the most dominant in the world and we should stick with it. He was right.

Most of the dismissals were done without severance pay (we literally had no cash) and were effective immediately. At this point, there was no one left in the company who was unaware of the financial problems, so dismissals had been expected by many. And my meetings with the fired employees were candid. It was impossible to think of them being any other way.

The lesson we left with was that dirty work is like any other dirt: It stays with you, and on you, until you've washed yourself of it. That's why you attack it with an energy that seems almost frantic. The longer dirt is in the air, the more likely people will come to believe it is part of the environment.

HONESTY IS YOUR DEBT TO PEOPLE IN A CRISIS

Even those who are lost to a crisis usually understand and accept the bad news as long as it is truthful. Honesty is an absolute, fundamental pillar of business relationships, even when that honesty causes pain.

It is when you try to hedge, to shade, to obscure, to cover up favoritism or pet projects, that you begin treading in quicksand. People detest few things so much as being lied to.

Most understood that what was being done was sheerly out of necessity. There were exceptions, of course. A rock was thrown at me during one meeting. There were several threats of litigation. My brother Jerry, who had the great misfortune to resemble me, was roughed up a bit outside the office building when he came for a visit. Still, these were exceptions during some extremely trying circumstances.

The dire shortage of cash in the enterprise put both us and some employees in tough spots. There was no money for severance, much less vacation pay and golden parachutes. To outsiders, it looked like a lot of bloodshed. In three days, we had decided to close several subsidiaries, disband eighteen computer centers, and dismiss 740 people. To the uninformed, I was the biggest scourge of Atlanta since William Tecumseh Sherman.

The next order of business was to revitalize the survivors.

In any reorganization, any shakeup, any crisis, there are casualties and survivors. Sometimes it will be only one or two individuals who are affected, but the same rules apply. You analyze; you plan; you strike; you bury your dead; and then you focus on the survivors. It is your relationship with them—and only them—that will make the crisis vanish and move the company ahead.

To the casualties you owe the truth and as much fairness as you can afford and they deserve.

BUILD THE TIGER'S DEN FROM DAY ONE

The real cultivation of business relationships begins the day you walk into a crisis, not when the dirty work is done. Those critical early relationships, in fact, will help you through it.

Dirty work comes in every shape imaginable in business. No one enjoys it, but it is one of the business jungle's permanent tenants. In the end, it's the implied promise to the survivors that says you deal with it whenever necessary. You do the job. Our operating phrase for two decades was: *whatever it takes.*

One thing it took was a tiger's den. The good news is that you can build a tiger's den—the key support group—from day one to help you. The den is inhabited by people who either are tigers themselves or who understand and appreciate Jungle Rules and the mentality of business tigers. When you're faced with either opportunity or crisis, the den is your first choice and your last resort.

Some of your early inductees into the den will stand out like a candle in a cave. For us, the most important was a shy, affable fellow in accounting by the name of Ivan Sigmund "Sig" Mosley. When we took over MSA, record keeping in the company was a disaster. Finding answers to some questions was like trying to reassemble shredded paper. I doubt that Kelly or I could have done it had we not come upon Sig.

Gene Kelly:

We went down to do some research and that's when I first met Sig Mosley. Until then I'd only had financials that had been produced for the creditors, but now I needed details. I asked the accounting department, and Sig raised his hand. Later I needed something else, and Sig raised his hand again. The man had the answers. After a while I didn't give a damn who was boss of a department, I went to Sig for the answers. Half an hour later, he had everything I needed.

Almost a quarter century later, Sig still is with me. And he still has all the answers.

You've got to find the Sig Mosleys of the company before the ink dries on your new business card. They give you answers, stability, performance, and insight *immediately,* and you can build the rest of your den from that critical core.

Sig was the wizard with books and numbers. You also need the rainmakers, the sales closers who almost pathologically refuse to let chaos, change, or trauma disrupt their tireless and confident selling.

The early den also needs product guardians—in our case, technical people willing to forget the concept of working hours and make sure the rainmakers had something to sell. From day one, you have to build it, sell it, and administer it. It might take three people or thirty or three thousand. But these, to steal the sports phrase, are the "go-to" bunch. The first tigers.

When you're populating the den, don't just look inside the company. You have to develop relationships with people on the outside who will influence your success. They might be suppliers whose wares you need, bankers whose credit is important, or—as in our case—lawyers and judges who held the absolute power of life and death over us.

The cutbacks at MSA were done on a Wednesday, Thursday, and Friday. On the following Monday, March 22, 1971, we began round two of the dirty work: We filed bankruptcy under Chapter X of the National Bankruptcy Act. Interestingly enough, it was in bankruptcy court that I got another lesson about people. Without the people who oversaw MSA's financial reorganization—Judges Newell Edenfield and A. D. Kahn; trustee Robert Hicks; attorney Ted Maloof—MSA would have ceased to exist.

What set our situation apart from other bankruptcies was that we were trying to give birth to a brand-new industry, the application software products business. We had to somehow make these nontechnical people believe that we had an idea worth preserving— and that preserving it was better for the world than liquidating the assets for insistent creditors.

Back then, it wasn't an easy sell. With the wrong people, it would have been an impossible one. Imagine someone coming to you today and telling you to believe in them because they had devised a method of transportation that was going to be ten times faster, ten times cheaper, and in ten years be used by everybody to whom mobility was important. And when you asked to see this device, they held up—nothing.

When I took the company into bankruptcy, I wasn't just faced with convincing judges, trustees, and lawyers that we were onto something. Almost everyone I knew told me we were a failure. The computer industry, once respectful of MSA, now viewed it as a casualty. Lending institutions would have nothing to do with us. Even my mother once took me aside and suggested firmly that I get a *real* job.

They said this because bankruptcy per se was considered a sign of failure. And, statistically, there was some reason to agree with that. At that time, something like two in a hundred companies that filed for bankruptcy reorganization actually turned things around. To build this den that would improve our odds, I needed to trudge door to door to sell this scenario to tigers.

The first thing you do in building this support group is identify its priority members—the movers, the shakers, the life-and-death makers. Then you figure out what their goals are and how to share them. Clearly the first elements of support for us had to be from the legal community.

Outside of MSA, the first door I was looking at was Judge Newell Edenfield's. Edenfield was this sort of judicial icon of the South, a man who had handed down key civil rights decisions in the mid '60s. This was a man who spoke with great eloquence and in capital letters.

His first act was to appoint a trustee, Robert E. Hicks, an Atlanta lawyer with a spun-honey voice and easy manner who could charm the teeth out of a shark. To this day he doesn't know exactly what software is, but he ended up being utterly instrumental in MSA's survival. If he didn't understand software, he at least understood us, believed in us, and came to share our goals. His first question to me showed he was open to taking on the challenge.

"Can we make this thing work?" he asked.

Those were exactly the words we needed to hear—"Can *we* make this thing work?" In that plural pronoun there was the basis for a relationship.

Before the courtroom proceedings began, we met with Judge Edenfield in his chambers. He asked essentially the same question. "Can this venture survive?"

"We have the support of the creditors," I said. "They are forgiving their debt for equity. We can get the company out and pay off the debt a little at a time."

"Tell me what software is," demanded Edenfield.

I explained that it was the method by which instructions and information were processed in a computer.

"You mean you sell the fizz off the Alka-Seltzer," he said. "Well, if you and Hicks tell me you can do this, let's go out and do it."

Again—"*Let's* go out and do it."

I had the first two non-MSA members of the den. I learned they shared the same goal: They wanted the bankruptcy reorganization to succeed, with no more harm to the secured creditors. Their fidelity was first to the creditors and not to MSA. As long as we shared that goal, they would give us the latitude to operate.

Over the next year and a half, Edenfield and Hicks delivered on their belief in us time and again. As we gave them small victories, they gave us more latitude. They stopped litigation that would have shut us down. When we asked for money for some seemingly odd promotions—a waterbed for a model to pose on at a bankers' convention in San Francisco, for example (more on this later)—they believed in us enough to come through. They achieved their goal, and we achieved ours, because we had agreed to share them. The tiger's den was making it happen.

JUNGLE RULE SUMMARY

A FIGHT TO THE LAST PERSON HAS NO WINNER.

Know exactly what you're fighting for and exactly what constitutes a victory, even if you don't know exactly how you're going to get it.

DIRTY WORK IS BEST DONE CLEANLY

Don't run from dirty work, grab it by the throat.

JUNGLE RULES

HONESTY IS YOUR DEBT TO PEOPLE IN A CRISIS

If you can't tell the truth, you can't lead.

BUILD THE TIGER'S DEN FROM DAY ONE

Find the "go to" team immediately.

4

MOTIVATING THE TIGERS

Jungle Rule #4:
Concentrate on the survivors.

Crises have more flashing red lights than a five-alarm fire at a police station. Distractions are ubiquitous. There is pressure from every quarter to divert your attention from your business's central problem, whatever it might be. But you can't allow that to happen. You need to execute the plan you've laid out in a strike, then through all the distractions you must *concentrate on the survivors.*

It's not easy. I remember after we severed those 740 people, the newspapers started calling me "The Butcher of Peachtree." That wasn't the epitaph I particularly wanted on my tombstone, assuming Atlantans would even allow me to be interred within their city limits. But we didn't let ourselves be pressed into second-guessing. Our single-minded focus was crucial to keeping the survivors—key people all—intact.

A moment amid the red lights of crisis: After we filed bankruptcy, our West Coast representative, Howard Smith, got a lucrative job offer from Computer Sciences Corporation, a prestigious company. I'd already learned enough about Howard to know I needed him in the den. He was a phenomenal salesman who was brilliant at building relationships, thinking creatively, and "making business happen" in unconventional ways. He was young, energetic, and unafraid of risks. I wanted to concentrate on him, to talk him into staying. Naturally, he shows up to talk to me about his job offer at the height of craziness in the office.

Fired employees are leaving. The sheriff is coming in with stickers and putting them on the furniture. Some unhappy people are shouting obscenities at me. The phone is ringing with lawyers and creditors. "Howard, you don't want to quit," I told him over the tempest. "I'm going to turn this thing around. Just sit there and watch."

I picked up one of the ringing phones. As if things couldn't get any worse, it was the ex-wife of one of the bank executives who had been dismissed over the loaning of the money to MSA. She was clearly inebriated and said she had a gun, which she explained to me was an Ira Johnson six-shot pistol, and she was "gonna shoot that SOB," meaning her ex.

"Ma'am," I pleaded, "you don't want to shoot him. It was just business."

"I just wanted to talk to the man who got him," she said, a little threateningly.

"I didn't *get* him," I said. "I'm a nice fellow, he's a nice fellow, we're all working to try to solve this problem." But she kept talking about ventilating him. I could hear the revolver clicking in the background, but I kept on talking. Finally she edged away from thoughts of homicide.

"You're a nice man," she eventually said (whew!). "Besides, I wasn't going to shoot him anyway. I couldn't hit him in his teeny, tiny tallywhacker." I almost fell out of the chair.

I had no idea what Howard was thinking, but it was easy to imagine he couldn't wait to call on CSC, where probably no one was fanning a six-shooter. I could have told him to meet me later, when things were saner. But even in that chaos—maybe *especially* in that chaos—I needed him to know we wanted him *now*. "This," I told him, "is a company that needs you. Stay with us."

"If you stay," he replied, "I'll stay."

Given what he'd witnessed, that was something only a tiger would say.

DON'T LEAVE YOUR WOUNDED ON THE BATTLEFIELD

Motivation is like love: The head may be involved, but the heart usually rules. People need an emotional fire from within as much as a logical one from above. Some people, the natural tigers, just never lose that emotional fire. It's an eternal flame. In others it has to be kindled. In still others it can't be found. But if both the intellectual and emotional fires can't be lit, no one will motivate themselves or be motivated by anyone else. What you end up with is unrequited business. Especially in tough times.

The truth is simple: If you can't motivate the survivors of a business crisis—including employees, prospects, and the market-place—you won't survive yourself. And after a crisis, you don't have long to do it. You need your people's heads to deliver your message and their hearts to deliver success.

You need hooks—drama, urgency, humor—to get their attention; you need clarity, honesty, and imagination to keep it; and you need to understand, and be willing to share, their goals. Motivation is that simple and that complex.

Motivation starts with the most fundamental Jungle Rule of all: *People are the key.* If you believe that product is the key—or packaging, or advertising, or market segmentation, or cellular phones for salesmen, or color fax machines, or faster personal computers—consider Alexander the Great, who would have been a spectacular businessman.

A student of Aristotle, Alexander assumed the reins of the Macedonian army at the age of sixteen. Despite his youth, he had a vision (Macedonian expansion) and surrounded himself with trained and devoted officers. He "hooked" his army by firing their imaginations with Aristotle's images of a world empire resting on Greek culture and traditions, with Macedonia as the capital. In battle, he kept their loyalty with one conspicuous practice: He never left his wounded soldiers behind. The soldiers rewarded him with inspired battles and ended up conquering every army that got in their way, even when they were vastly outnumbered.

Now that was management.

In the end, people almost always respond when they believe they won't be left behind. It's at this point that business evolves from a collection of people into a fraternity and from there into a family—the formal name for a group of tigers.

ATTACK THE DOUBTS

When we looked at the survivors of MSA and thought about what would prevent their full and energetic participation in our rebirth, doubt came back. It was that throat we had to go for.

After the takeover and bankruptcy, Gene Kelly and I were looking at a three-headed dragon: We had to revitalize the company for the remaining employees; we had to reestablish our name to a doubtful industry; and we had to re-interest frightened buyers. We had few employees, no money, no borrowing power, and a watchful court. It was a motivational nightmare and the cause of much understandable doubt.

The company's fabric was tissue thin. We had kept a nucleus of key people to launch this venture, but many were wary of being fired themselves or were emotionally depleted by the reorganization. A company they had been told would become "the IBM of software" had been decimated. Old goals and visions lay in ruins about them. And here were Kelly and Imlay trying to convince this group of people of this bold, new idea about the future of computing.

The first act of motivation—the first strike at doubt—was to tell them that we had only one shoe; a second wasn't going to drop. We figured morale could begin to rebound if people were certain a second wave of firings wasn't coming. That's why we executed the plan with what some thought was brutal quickness, dismissing 740 people in a strike. We knew morale and motivation would be completely unsalvageable if there was even a second round of dismissals. That was the first point we stressed in meetings with the survivors. And from there on, we said that we were with them as long as they were with us. Like Alexander the Great's troops, no member of this new army would be left behind. But not everyone believed us.

Harry Howard:

The first time I saw John, he came into a meeting with Gene Kelly. We had heard that Kelly was the hatchet man for John. They said if given the chance, he'd slit your throat. There were some fifty people in the meeting. John was standing in the front and Kelly was at his side. We all knew the troubles. Then John gave what I later learned was a typical John speech. "We all need to hang in and do our jobs and stick together—we'll come out of it. We'll make it go. I have the confidence. There is a business here." He didn't overpromise. He said there would be rough times and he needed our support. Most of the people in the meeting—those on the sales and technical side— seemed antagonistic toward John. Bebe Whitaker, a young lady on the General Ledger staff, stood up and called him a liar.

There is only one way for managers to really overcome criticism that borders on hostility: You have to lead by example. As President Eisenhower used to say, "You can't move a rope by pushing it." You lead. After you talk the talk, you walk the walk. But we had to talk the talk first. We had to communicate our vision and our plan to get there. If we didn't, this train would never leave the station.

We not only needed these people, we needed an unprecedented effort from them. We needed them to be more than they ever had been in the old MSA. We needed them to be extraordinary. We needed them to become tigers. And we needed them to believe we shared their goals.

Because we had an audience that was largely Georgian, we used familiar imagery to show them our plan—and to hook them with flair. We put together a fun slide presentation called "Bankruptcy Ain't So Bad," using scenes from the movie *Gone With the Wind* to illustrate MSA's rebirth.

The burning of Atlanta was used to represent the collapse. The famous street scene of dead and wounded soldiers represented the people we'd lost. Then came reconstruction. At the end, Rhett and Scarlett were locked in an embrace, symbolizing the way we would take care of our customers. The humor we used in the presentations took the edge off our people's fears. For these Georgians, the images really hit home. And they believed in nothing so much as their ability to rise from the ashes.

One time they almost literally had to do that. I called everyone in to give them a motivational talk about our sales goals. To dramatize the idea of "firing up," I lit some papers soaked in accelerant and threw them into a trash can. The fire got out of control in an instant, catching the drapes on fire and sending everyone running into the street. Fire trucks came screaming up and put out the blaze. Fortunately, there wasn't a lot of damage to anything except my reputation as a fire handler. Shortly thereafter, we dropped pyrotechnics from our list of motivational tools (although I note that we exceeded sales goals after that meeting). We adopted animals instead, which we found also sometimes went up draperies, but never exploded into flame.

PEOPLE ARE THE KEY

The jungle is rife with symbols of worship. Sometimes it's gold statuary, other times a volcano. In the movie *The Gods Must Be Crazy,* it was a Coke bottle. In effect, these icons are touchstones for people to remind themselves of why they are there and where they should be going.

In the business jungle, it's also possible to acquire a lot of symbols. Marketing will conceive its share. Department heads will use their own. Annual kick-off dinners should have their themes for the year. But amid all the more transient symbols, there should be one icon—and one message—that endures, like the billion-year-old volcano. One that becomes the essence of the company soul.

For MSA, that symbol was a key. And the simple message was: *People are the key.*

We wanted people, above all else, to know that we believed in them; that we sincerely felt that they—not technology, though we were in a technology business—were the key to whatever this company was going to become. We knew this was a message that a lot of companies used. It certainly wasn't original with MSA. But we also knew that saying it and delivering on it were vastly different things. Like a lot of things in life (and business), the secret to success is *execution.* That was where we could make the message meaningful.

For our "volcano," we of course went to Tiffany's. Bill Graves and I reasoned that a tangible symbol for MSA's central message had to be of high quality. When we spoke with the jeweler, he showed us this small, elegant pin in the shape of an old pipekey. It was a perfect symbol.

"How much is it?" asked Graves.

"Ninety-eight dollars," the jeweler told him.

Graves looked taken aback. "Do you have anything that's gold-*plated?*"

"Sir," the jeweler hissed dryly, "this is *Tiffany's!*"

That settled it. We took the keys.

That key remained our symbol of commitment to people. Men were given small lapel keys; women received larger pins. For those with up to five years with the company, the pins were silver; after that they were gold.

Once we'd had a chance to prove that "People are the key" wasn't just sloganeering, the keys became objects of surprising emotion. People who lost them were frantic. There were moments when we really understood how profoundly people had come to associate the key with the company. We once had to dismiss one young woman in Hong Kong. A few days later we received the key in the mail. Even though it was valuable, and we never asked for them back, she couldn't dissociate it from the company.

The keys were a source of great pride. I once encountered a fellow whose pin was missing, which was like coming to work without your pants. "Where's your pin?" I asked teasingly.

He thought for a moment, then answered, "I must have left it on my pajamas."

The key also came to represent our relationships with customers.

One of our fiercest competitors, McCormack & Dodge Corporation, came to detest the keys so much that they created "Keybuster Awards" for any salespersons who beat out MSA. We figured we must be doing something right to get that kind of reaction, and it only increased our emphasis on people.

While McCormack & Dodge stressed leading-edge technology in its marketing, MSA stressed people, goal sharing, customer satisfaction, and the personal touch. In every year of our head-to-head competition, MSA won in sales and market share. Thus the keys became tangible—and motivational—symbols that were part of every sales call.

In 1990, after MSA was sold to Dun & Bradstreet and merged with McCormack & Dodge (which D & B then owned), we dropped the key symbol because it was such a touchy icon for the McCormack & Dodge employees. Every once in a while, though, I'd pass someone in the hallway. We might not even speak, but he would flip his lapel over briefly to reveal the key on the underside, then pass on by with a smile.

But in those early days, we still had to prove ourselves, to walk the walk. A lot of companies say they emphasize people, but don't really follow up. That wasn't a trap we intended to step in. Which is why the second step in attacking doubt is to demonstrate by your example why it shouldn't exist.

PEOPLE LISTEN TO WORDS, BUT FOLLOW EXAMPLES

One of the most important distinctions I ever made was between teaching and telling. I learned early on that anyone can tell, but leaders can teach. And the best way to teach was by example. So "Teach, don't tell" became one of the mottos I adopted for myself.

Think for a moment about the phrase "Follow the leader." It doesn't say, "Do what the leader says" or "Follow the memo" or "Let's check with the palm reader." It says *follow the leader.*

If you're the leader, that means you have to be willing to hit the beach with the troops. You can't lead anyone from a bunker in the rear.

At MSA, I was asking our salespersons to go out into the field for a company that was very publicly bankrupt, was being knocked horribly by the competition, and was financed solely by daily sales. Because sales was my principal background, and because I was the one articulating MSA's new direction in speeches, I was often asked to go on sales calls. I went every opportunity I got—and I still do.

I especially liked trying to turn around situations that seemed irreversible. With that you can show leadership, and the stories make their way back through the grapevine. If the salesperson gets his commission for something he thought he'd lost, the news races through the organization faster than the fire that went up the draperies.

It's especially useful when the salespersons see you color outside the lines, so to speak, take a little initiative, be a little creative. If I wanted them to play by rules that liberate them, I could motivate them by my example.

All of the salespersons knew they could call me. They usually didn't do it unless they had a problem, so I had a lot of chances to lead by example. I once got a call from a new, young account executive named Warren Weiss, who was having a problem with a client at a gas company in Indianapolis. I flew there, walked in, and the customer said, "I don't want your product, I don't want you, I don't want this guy around anymore. Can't stand him. It's too bad because your features and functions are right, but I don't want to do any business with you."

Warren had made every mistake a young salesman could make, including going over the head of the customer, then saying some indelicate things about him to his superior.

The first thing I did was ask Warren to leave, at least until I could calm down the customer. Then I sat down with the customer and said, "You want the product. Let's try to get it done." He looked doubtfully at me, then decided to see if there was any substance.

"We need a full technical evaluation," he told me.

I picked up the phone and called MSA's top technician and had him fly in there that night. The customer gathered his staff, and we met in a hotel until one in the morning, evaluating the gas company's situation and what we could do to solve its technical problems and identify and share its goals. We sent Warren out to bring us pizza and beer, but made sure he was in on what personal service really meant in the field, which was: *whatever it takes.*

The meeting opened his eyes. Here was his customer being supported personally by the company president and the top technical guy, talking about technology and goals and personal commitment, all in the middle of the night, six hundred miles from headquarters. The next morning the customer signed a contract worth $500,000. It was Warren's first contract.

Warren not only kept the customer, he rose to become MSA's top salesman, then top district manager, top regional manager, operations manager, and eventually a vice president. Today he's the head of field operations at Next Computer.

You don't leave your wounded on the battlefield. You're with them whenever they need you, leading from the front.

HOW TO TURN CRISES INTO SELLING POINTS

And you thought crisis had no value.

One of the biggest hurdles for our motivation program was getting salespersons comfortable with selling the software of a company in bankruptcy. They were going into battle with competitors who took every opportunity to tell prospects that MSA was destitute, groping for a few dollars just before liquidation, and would leave them in the lurch.

In meetings, we could get their heads with creative explanations of what our plan was and how good our software was, but we needed their hearts for face-to-face selling. We got them by showing them how to turn a wart into a beauty mark.

If people could turn bankruptcy into an asset, we figured they could sell anything, probably forever. The unconquerable tiger. And they would never again lose their motivation for some perceived "liability." There would be no problem they could not recast as an opportunity. They would, in effect, be liberated from negative thinking.

But how do you turn bankruptcy into an asset?

It occurred to us that Judge Edenfield, this historic judicial figure who was profoundly respected everywhere, was in essence in charge of the company. He was, for all intents and purposes, putting the guarantee of the federal bench on MSA's software. It was saying, "This deal is okay because I'm watching this company with a microscope, and I think they are going to make it."

A little imagination led us outside the old rules.

We developed an idea that explained to prospects that bankruptcy *wasn't* bad (thus the title of the presentation we made to them). To continue as MSA was before would have been bad. But the bankruptcy freed us to focus solely on software products and the customers who used them. Bankruptcy was good. Bankruptcy liberated us. Bankruptcy purged us, healed us, and focused us. And to top it off, a federal judge will sign the contract.

Howard Smith:

It was maybe a matter of where I wasn't smart enough to realize this bankruptcy was a problem. When I called the office, they said, "We've got some bad news: MSA just filed bankruptcy." My comment was: "Jeez, do I still get paid?" John told me, "Keep on selling!" I remember one of the first sales we closed in bankruptcy was Walt Disney. I was sitting in the meeting and the controller said, "We understand you're in bankruptcy." And I said, "Yes, but that's good news for you," and turned it around to be very positive. And I really saw it as a great opportunity from a customer standpoint. It was John who said to tell people, "This software absolutely works because it's been approved by the court and the court wouldn't let us sell it if it didn't work." There was no reason they wouldn't buy from us just because we were in bankruptcy. As a matter of fact, I think the year we were in bankruptcy was the year I was top salesman.

Over the year and a half we were in bankruptcy reorganization, the court's imprimatur became one of MSA's strongest selling points. In August of 1972, we found out just how strong. The *Wall Street Journal* wrote that MSA was about to emerge from bankruptcy. The day the article appeared, we had six deals that closed immediately.

It was all a master stew of motivation. The salespersons genuinely believed in their product, believed they could sell it, and believed that MSA was going to survive and prosper. The judge was motivated to do everything he could to help the venture succeed. And the clients were motivated to pick up some good software with an unusual warranty. It was what happens when people share goals.

And it drove our competition nuts.

"LOOK AT ME, LISTEN TO ME, FOLLOW ME"

We now were succeeding in one-on-one selling. But we needed to pursue bigger prey. The second stage of our motivation plan was to motivate prospects into becoming customers and to do it en masse. We decided early on that trying to obscure our financial situation wasn't the way to go. As Henry Kissinger observed after Watergate, "Anything that will be revealed eventually, should be revealed immediately."

The other way to go was to publicize it. What we were having salespersons say in private, face-to-face meetings with prospects, we needed to say to the world at large. Not in fine print, but in bold headlines. Doing so would take away a weapon from our competitors, who could not tell prospects about the "dirty little secret" we were hiding.

Thus the next stage was to go from private to public forums; to move from motivating individual prospects to look at us, to motivating masses of them to do it. We knew we had an important, even compelling, story to tell. But getting masses to turn out to listen to the tales of a company with a "history"—we were known back then as "the company that cost First National Bank all of its profits in 1970"—was the trick.

Most software companies were run by technicians; their marketing was informative, but technical, straightforward, and bland. I love technicians, God bless their little bytes. They're wonderful people, and the world needs them. But many are very literal, very specific, in their wording and thinking. In another context, they would never bound into a saddle when they could insert the left foot into the left-side stirrup, extend the left leg at the knee, and so on. You get the picture.

But computing was already changing the business world. It was becoming less a dialogue among technicians and more of a discussion among businesspersons. We thought people were ready for talks about computing as a competitive weapon, as a productivity tool, as executive support, as a profit tool. We thought they were ready for color, for metaphor, for flair. We didn't have anything at stake but the company.

It was about this time that we came up with the single most pivotal idea in MSA's renaissance. It was a great lesson in the value of gratitude when properly expressed.

We decided to thank the banks that were buying our software. Thus was born the theme "Thanks to Banks," a three-word juggernaut that spawned a complete reversal of MSA's troubled image—and did it in a matter of days.

We had little money and a lot of chutzpah. But imagination, in the scheme of things, has always been more important than money. We realized that no one, in our memories, had ever formally thanked banks for anything. It was like thanking lawyers. It had never been done.

The question was how should we couch our thank you. We needed to be eye-catching, so we decided to put the message on a waterbed, which was a relatively new innovation at the time. We took the symbol for "Full-Service Banking"—a blue circle with a white ring on the edge—and replaced the words with "Thanks to Banks."

We printed up some badges with the message on them and took the whole package out to San Francisco to an American Bankers Association convention. Then we hired a model to pose on the waterbed with the bankers. (She would sit on the edge, they next to her.) We hired a photographer to immortalize the moment for the bankers, who left our booth with a badge, some MSA literature, and a memory of the company that wouldn't soon leave them.

Then the unexpected happened. Our $5,000 booth (including travel) was drawing in more people than IBM's $4 million booth. The "Thanks to Banks" message found its way to the banner that hung over the entrance to the convention center. Downtown hotel marquees that had been sporting other messages suddenly picked up on "Thanks to Banks." We had to do a rush reorder of buttons because they vanished in a day. Newspapers picked up the theme as if it had been conceived by the convention organizers.

Before it was over practically every conference attendee had come by for a button and a photo. I honestly don't think anyone stayed away. Overnight, we had delivered a message, in a fun way, that stuck like glue to representatives of banks from all over America.

And no one was asking about our bankruptcy reorganization. Not a soul cared. We had become the "Thanks to Banks" company. Afterward, when we went on sales calls, we only had to mention "Thanks to Banks" (we wore the button on sales calls) and there was instant recognition of MSA. We used the concept for three years. It never failed to be a smash hit.

But what was most important to MSA was what "Thanks to Banks" had done for us in the days after that initial show. We had used an inexpensive idea with a sincere message, had a little fun with it, and received millions of dollars of positive publicity and image reformation. I'm not even sure it would have been possible to buy the image change we enjoyed with any amount of money—if the message had missed the mark.

We had gotten people to look at MSA, always the first step in turning prospects into clients. And an amazing thing began to happen: We started to sell better than before we were in bankruptcy.

EVERY GREAT IDEA HAS NINE LIVES

Creativity doesn't always mean coming up with an entirely new concept. Sometimes it means imaginatively evolving an existing idea that works.

Our next step was to motivate even more prospects to listen to the MSA story—to move from hundreds to thousands. The "Thanks to Banks" campaign had been an astounding success. We also worked with Fran Tarkenton as a celebrity draw at customer conferences we held—conferences where we were trying to present our ideas about software as a competitive weapon to high-level bank executives. They turned out in droves for Tarkenton, and were, as we'd thought, extremely interested in our message.

We began to wonder how many lives the idea could have. How

many manifestations could we effectively devise without getting stale? The answer was: a lot.

We contracted with Tarkenton to do a series of ads that spoofed the athlete ads of the day. He would be pictured with his face covered in shaving cream below the headline: "Not shaving cream, Fran—General Ledger!" We did it with coffeemakers, rental cars, everything but Joe Namath's pantyhose (he refused).

And if the evolution of ideas is good, they don't lose steam over time. One of the last of Tarkenton's nine lives with us was a promotion we did to give away his Super Bowl tickets. We had more than eighteen thousand responses.

Like the "Thanks to Banks" campaign, this campaign created a tremendously strong image for MSA. Our corporate identity sky-rocketed. Every ad carried the message of "Scrambling and Winning." Technical purists, used to seeing ads picturing terminals or printouts, wondered aloud why a "software company" would try to tie shaving cream into technology messages—and why people were motivated to respond.

But we didn't portray ourselves as "selling software"; we were a people company scrambling to solve business problems, and software was incidentally a tool we used. And people were motivated to respond because they didn't "buy software" just to have it; they had competitive problems or information problems or other business problems that needed to be solved.

Over the years we stayed with the idea of celebrity draws, using such athletes as Dick Butkus, Frank Gifford, Paul Hornung, and Tommy Lasorda, such political figures as Gerald Ford and Henry Kissinger, and business gurus like Peter Drucker.

They were always people who were achievers, who were successful, who had reached the top of their game—the image we wanted people to have of MSA. People would sit in rapt attention and come away feeling they owed you something for arranging for them to rub elbows with a hero of theirs. It gave us a competitive edge.

Then, of course, having hooked them ("look at me"), you had

to keep them with a compelling story ("listen to me"), and then convince them you could help them reach their goals ("follow me").

We had that story. We had believed so feverishly in the future of software products, in each other, and in our company that prospects got caught up in our motivated enthusiasm. And success bred success.

Tom Walker, *Atlanta Journal,* October 26, 1971:

Management Science America, Inc. (MSA), an Atlanta-based computer software firm, has moved in the last six months toward a rare goal in American business: a successful emergence from a Chapter X bankruptcy ... In that time, MSA has added some blue-chip clients ranging from Boeing Computer Services; Walt Disney Productions; Merrill Lynch, Pierce, Fenner and Smith; Paine, Webber, Jackson and Curtis; Kerr-McGee; Eli Lilly, Inc.; Coca-Cola Bottling of Los Angeles; and Playboy Enterprises (where MSA's software will handle the payroll for Playboy Bunnies). Altogether some fifty clients were added in the last half-year period.

JUNGLE RULE SUMMARY

CONCENTRATE ON THE SURVIVORS.

Lives are determined by the living.

DON'T LEAVE YOUR WOUNDED ON THE BATTLEFIELD

Once a tiger is in the family, never leave him in trouble.

ATTACK THE DOUBTS

Learn what fosters discontent, then kill it in its tracks.

PEOPLE ARE THE KEY

Make sure employees and customers understand that your belief in people isn't a slogan, but a pillar of your business.

PEOPLE LISTEN TO WORDS, BUT FOLLOW EXAMPLES

You can't lead a rope by pushing it.

HOW TO TURN CRISES INTO SELLING POINTS

If you can sell bankruptcy, you can sell anything.

"LOOK AT ME, LISTEN TO ME, FOLLOW ME"

Motivating customers to buy from you means getting their attention with creativity, entrenching them with a message of substance, then delivering tirelessly on your promise.

EVERY GREAT IDEA HAS NINE LIVES

Learn to evolve ideas as well as people.

5

Jungle Rule #5:
Don't be afraid of whatever it takes.

Brent Wells, who was a longtime sales manager at MSA, once was talking about the lengths MSA's tigers would go to accomplish a mission. "The British Army," he reminded us, "had no formal code of conduct. We didn't either. We just had integrity." He was talking about the notion at MSA of doing *whatever it takes* to get a job done.

Whatever it takes. Business tigers, I've learned, never are intimidated by the challenge of doing whatever it takes. It's really more of an instinct with them, one that's either cultivated or stifled by company policy.

Whatever it takes is a liberating theme in the jungle. It's not about playing dirty—our explicit charge at MSA was to do whatever it took, as long as it was legal, ethical, and moral—but about adapting to any situation in order to win. *Whatever it takes* was our common understanding that we were in business to succeed at it, and it would take a pretty savage and determined enemy to stop us.

We used *whatever it takes* in selling (goal sharing), in customer service (any employee available, any hour, any day, for any problem) and product support (maintenance and enhancement), and in just plain survival tactics.

Wells remembers, "We used to travel four days a week, eat no lunch, work eighteen-hour days, then walk into a presentation looking like we had just stepped off a wedding cake. We had to."

In retrospect, if we hadn't had that mentality, MSA would have died within weeks of our taking it over. With conventional rules, people draw a line that says: this much and no more. It's a kind of quota system. They allocate a certain number of methods to make the contact. A certain number of calls to make the sale. A certain number of support people to solve problems. A certain number of working hours to fine-tune things. A certain sacrifice they won't make.

Whatever it takes dispensed with all of that. If it was legal, moral, and ethical, there was little MSA's tigers wouldn't do to keep the jungle from consuming them. Especially in the bankruptcy days, when we were constrained by the courts, assaulted by competitors, and questioned by customers who weren't sure we'd survive, *whatever it takes* gave us the charter to persist—to imagine a little longer, to create a little better, to pursue a little more doggedly, and to sacrifice battles to win the war.

Take money. As someone once said, "Happiness is positive cash flow." When we first took MSA's reins, we had no money. We were totally without funds. Our bank account had been garnished by creditors. Most of our assets had been encumbered. We needed cash to pay the remaining employees to keep them from leaving, but everything had been locked up as if we were being ordained to fail. And if we couldn't meet payroll, we were cooked.

That's when we decided to do our own interpretation of which assets were encumbered. Using this technique, we found some expensive antique furniture and paintings—remnants of the lavish days—that we decided were not legally bound to anyone, probably because no one had found them. We used them to get a loan to make a $52,000 payroll. Saved for another week.

Later, our bankruptcy agreement with Judge Edenfield's court said that we had to make payroll each week or the entire operation would be folded. We were doing everything imaginable—whatever it took—to make cash sales and get the money in. But the software business back then was notoriously erratic—some months would see a half-million dollars in sales, others nothing—and our financial situation only compounded problems.

At one point, we were in a dry stretch where money hadn't come in weeks. Our agreement said that every Monday morning at 9 A.M. there would be enough money to pay everyone by that Friday. We survived that way for about a year. Then one Monday we didn't have it; and there was no pending sale on the horizon that would correct things by Friday. We didn't want to let a year of frantic effort go down the drain for one lost payday. What would it take?

We had been in litigation with a bank called the Trust Company of Georgia over the ownership of an extremely valuable software package that had been developed at MSA and used at the bank. It was the kind of software that a massive line of business could be built around. We had continued to do development work on the software, a stockholder accounting system, but the bank had licensed a New York company, Programming Methods, Inc., to market the software on behalf of the bank, a move we took issue with.

MSA had a compelling case—that the software really had been misappropriated, that the bank's rights to it had expired three years earlier, and that MSA had spent $405,000 on developing it after those rights had expired—but we had a payroll to meet on Friday. We would be liquidated before the case would be heard.

So you do *whatever it takes* to "be in position to be in position." We released the claims on the software in exchange for $100,000. We received the money on Thursday and made the Friday payroll. In doing whatever it took, we sacrificed a certain victory in court and relinquished a software product that later would be used to found another entire software company, Stockholder Systems, Inc. We abandoned the battle in order to win the war. No flinching.

That's what it takes.

CRISIS COLLECTIONS

During the bankruptcy there was some resistance to MSA's collections efforts for receivables. And this was when every penny in the door counted toward survival. Some of it came from the fact that some customers did not want to make payments to a company that "might momentarily fold" (as competitors were wont to tell them). Some of it derived from legitimate questions about who was going to finish works in progress, and when. And, in truth, a few reasoned that they could just wait out MSA's demise and walk off with some software.

There are certain lines you do not cross in collections—we wanted to build customer relationships, and threats and intimidation aren't the way to do that—but we needed to get whatever money was legitimately owed us—and fast. The question became: How do you show your claws without actually using them?

In most instances, simple candor was the best answer. We would explain our situation, our new direction, our focus on software products, and answer every question customers had about our chances for the future. We even put it all into a formal presentation with slides, humor, and our honest view of the future, and the tactic usually sufficed. But not everyone was convinced.

Gene Kelly, who spent his entire career at MSA without a formal title, was put in charge of shaking the bushes for much-needed cash. Bob Hicks, the trustee who was in effect the CEO of the company, gave Kelly the title of "assistant to the trustee" in order to put some weight behind Kelly's collections calls. Then he would hit the road knowing that if he failed, if we missed a payroll, we all could go down.

Early on, he called on United Virginia Bankshares, which had had a problem with where MSA stood on a software project that was almost, but not quite, completed. We wanted to make certain the customer was happy with the software, but we also didn't have time to drag out the receivables process.

Gene Kelly:

If someone disputed what they owed based on work in progress, I would have someone technically competent call that customer and talk to their technical person at length about what had been delivered and what we were in the process of shipping. This is what I did with UVB.

But they disputed the amount. I went there and said, "I'm the assistant trustee and I'm worried about getting a check in the mail. Maybe this forty thousand dollars is in dispute. Maybe you don't owe all of it. But it's my job to tell a federal judge that you owe MSA this forty thousand dollars. Now we have supplied a substantial portion of that work-in-progress and I've got to appear before Judge Edenfield next Friday"—I'm making this up at the time—"and tell him the story. If he's not happy, he'll want you and your lawyer to come explain it to him." We adjourned to the conference room and had a quiet meeting. I flew back with a check for forty thousand dollars.

Intimidating? Maybe a little. Kelly later told me it was amazing how effectively the grapevine works in the jungle. The story permeated the rest of the companies who owed us almost instantly. "I didn't have a hell of a lot of trouble collecting from most of the others," he said.

There is some danger in applying *whatever-it-takes* principles in the receivables business. You can risk looking like a repo outfit or knee-jerk litigator if your tactics don't have the elements of a long-term relationship in them. What Kelly had told UVB was true: They *would* have to appear before Judge Edenfield (though, truth be told, not that next Friday).

The line that we drew was a simple one: Even in desperation, we never asked for money that wasn't owed us. And once we were paid, we applied some lavish *whatever-it-takes* principles of customer service and technical support to make certain the client saw from the start that the money spent then—and whatever they spent later—was the best investment they could have made. We made certain that UVB's project was wrapped up by our top technicians as soon as Kelly returned.

UVB thereafter never had a solitary question about its investment. Good business is usually just a matter of keeping a promise.

IF YOU CAN'T STAND THE PRESSURE, GET OUT OF THE JUNGLE

One of the business jungle's most pervasive sounds is the clock. For some, it can be more intimidating than the combat screech of the fiercest predator. You can hear its tireless sound behind you at every turn, night and day. For others, its incessant ticking can be inspirational. It depends on how capably you handle pressure.

The jungle clock warns of impending deadlines, of quotas, of the closing of monthly books (and commissions), of annual bonus bogeys, of missed meetings, of late flights, and of a thousand other ticking crisis-opportunities. The jungle clock might be the greatest test of business tigers willing to play the game of *whatever it takes*.

One good example of this occurred when MSA's tax-loss carryforward was about to expire. After the bankruptcy was filed, we didn't have to pay corporate taxes; but when the carryforward expired, we were looking at a horrific rate of 50 cents on the dollar in taxes. So as the clock ticked toward the expiration date, we were trying to close as much business as humanly possible.

Dennis Vohs, who was then MSA's vice president of product development, had a massive deal presented to nine of twelve Federal Reserve Banks in New York City. It was a Tuesday and the carryforward was to expire at midnight Sunday. To make matters worse, Thursday was Thanksgiving, and everyone was going to shut down for the holiday. Vohs flew up because, while the banks liked the software, price had yet to be negotiated. And the clock was ticking.

Dennis Vohs:

We kept the terms relatively high because it was a high cost of sales and maintenance deal. We negotiated all day on Tuesday. On Wednesday, they had me in the bank, but wouldn't allow me in the conference room. But I could hear the hours of discussion. Then I heard the chairman of the board of governors say the deal wasn't priced right and I had until Monday to come back or bidding would be reopened. But Monday would be too late.

So I grabbed the Federal Reserve Bank of New York people and tried to come up with a satisfactory price for all parties. We finally agreed on some terms. It was two hundred and eighty thousand dollars. We called all the people right then and got the authorizations. But then they said they wouldn't pay us until they received the products and documentation and got an invoice, which usually takes a week. It was late on the Wednesday before Thanksgiving, and my wife was waiting for me in Florida with the kids.

So I left the bank, changed flights, flew back through Atlanta, dragged an assistant controller onto the plane, got the signed contract, took it to the office, wrote an invoice, copied all of the new documentation on the Xerox copier—eight copies, hundreds of pages—shipped everything back by air courier, and convinced them all to send the money on Saturday to beat the deadline by a few hours.

That gambit saved MSA several hundred thousand dollars. Whatever it takes. The clock stops for no one. And that was typical Vohs.

Another time, the Bank of New York was scheduled to go live with an MSA payroll system it had bought. Thousands of employees needed it to get paid. But at the last minute there was a glitch. It wouldn't take input and record the names and numerical information from the bank's tapes. It wasn't MSA's fault, but that didn't change the seriousness of the problem or the consequences of failing to figure something out.

So Vohs, without flinching, assembled a SWAT team of MSA people from Atlanta and New Jersey and, in one of the great speed-entry exercises in computing history, had them manually type hundreds of thousands of bits of payroll information into the system over the weekend. On Monday morning it went live, on schedule.

Customers never forget.

MAKE *WHATEVER IT TAKES* CONTAGIOUS

A year and a half after MSA filed bankruptcy in Atlanta, it emerged from that reorganization, freed by the court to fail or succeed on its own. One thing that became clear during those eighteen months was that the idea of *whatever it takes*—a notion you will see illustrated countless times in this book—is not merely the only way to survive a crisis, but the only way to run a company.

Individuals excel personally by doing whatever it takes, but companies excel when everyone is doing it. One of the joys of watching this mentality take root was the sense of confidence people began to feel, a confidence reflected in the selling, in the market contacts, in the expressions of confidence about the future. Forget that only two of a hundred companies successfully emerged from this bankruptcy. Everyone knew that the shackles were off, that the tigers had been uncaged, and that every chance to succeed was being explored.

Our business tigers, armed with their autonomy, always felt that they had the freedom to stalk creatively while alone in the field. Now they also knew that everyone in the company was doing the same thing—and that help, should it be needed, was ready to swarm to their aid.

The chemistry rubbed off on others associated with those crisis days. Customers began to regain confidence, girded by watching this strange group of people who might bring twelve people to a sales presentation—including the president—to make certain every concern was addressed. Judges Edenfield and Kahn ruled numerous times in our favor when old creditors wanted to shut down operations and liquidate. Bob Hicks, the trustee, gave us more and more latitude when he saw the tenacity with which we were trying to succeed. After a while it became clear that no one wanted to be the one who ruined what was going on.

And that became the lesson we carried into the next phase of the company's life. *Whatever it takes* was no longer a crisis policy, but a company policy. It would come to be the way we sold, marketed, supported, created, communicated, rewarded, and celebrated. The tigers were ready to run.

JUNGLE RULE SUMMARY

DON'T BE AFRAID OF *WHATEVER IT TAKES.*

No limits on creativity or commitment, as long as its legal, ethical, and moral.

CRISIS COLLECTIONS

Learn to show your claws without using them.

IF YOU CAN'T STAND THE PRESSURE, GET OUT OF THE JUNGLE

Tigers have to deal with a hundred time-oriented pressures.

MAKE *WHATEVER IT TAKES* CONTAGIOUS

If you've assembled the right people, the tiger mentality will sustain everyone around it.

Part II

RUNNING WITH THE TIGERS

*He who rides the tiger finds it
difficult to dismount.*
　　　　　　—Old Chinese saying

6

TRACKING DOWN THE TIGERS

Jungle Rule #6:
Never hunt for tigers just to put them on a leash.

As MSA emerged from bankruptcy reorganization, we knew we were onto something special. We'd taken the company from insolvency to a small ($205,000) profit in just eighteen months. Everyone sensed the momentum.

MSA's people, especially its salespeople, felt a kind of exuberance in the nascent software industry. They were like a small band of happy gunslingers—a label that later stuck to them—in the West's wildest days. The world was up for grabs.

But we also knew that most of the success we'd enjoyed had come from that core group of people who had survived the reorganization. If the company was to grow the way we'd envisioned—I'd brashly told them, "We're going to be the largest software company in the world"—we'd have to hunt down more tigers to bring into the family. We knew that the rules of business conduct—the Jungle Rules—we'd formulated to survive in the crisis days were going to be kept intact (after all, they had worked). But we also would need some new ones; ones that new hires could embrace and run with in this new era.

The question suddenly was: How do you find and hire tigers? That spawned more questions. Where do they come from? What is their educational profile? What is their industry experience? What do you ask in an interview? Are tigers born or made?

When we sat down to look at the characteristics of the tigers the company already had, it was hard coming up with a conventional profile. There was tremendous disparity among them. They had eclectic educational backgrounds (and grade point averages), widely varying grasps of technology, differing business experiences, and personality types that were all over the graph. There were few common denominators on the usual list of checkpoints, so we decided to look elsewhere.

What we found the group had in common were what turned out to be the key markers in the tiger hunt:

Tenacity

They were tenacious in the richest sense of the word. Tenacity isn't something usually taught in a classroom, but it is fundamentally there in people or fundamentally missing. It's probably genetic. In all business tigers it is fundamentally there. They don't give up on a sale, on a problem, on a challenge, on a roadblock, on a competitor. If they had this basic asset, then we could look next for those characteristics that supported tenacity, that allowed people to be *effectively* relentless. Those characteristics began with:

Energy

The only kind of person who can work without regard to the omnipresent clock is the high-energy individual. We looked for people who were so energized they could have lighted a city, which, metaphorically, was what we wanted them to do. Under the umbrella charge of doing *whatever it takes,* they had to be on call twenty-four hours a day. Tenacity needs energy before anything else.

Competitiveness

We found there was a strange and wonderful balance in the tigers. They loved to win just as much as they hated to lose. Not all people are that way, even some competitors. People might love to win, but are not uncomfortable with losing. We looked for people to whom losing was the bitterest of consequences.

Imagination

We needed people who could think on their feet, who could imagine on the fly new solutions to problems (how to meet an elusive contact, how to marshal scarce resources on a moment's notice, how to spontaneously move an audience of one or a thousand). Imagination was the missing ingredient in most of their competitors, who tended to be confined to by-the-book prescriptions in doing business. We also had a book, but we wanted people who would write in the margins.

Durability

We hunted people who would not get paralyzed after a setback. Tenacity requires the ability to be an intellectual and emotional fullback, hitting the line again and again until the opening is there. I'd seen in MSA's tigers a facility not to get down, at least not for long. They seemed to know a truth I discovered long ago: that *regret* never accomplished anything. Time spent lamenting a setback is time lost overcoming it.

Courage

They had to think a level above the conventional. They had to be courageous enough to ask questions such as: "Just why *can't* we get a U.S. president to close some sales for us?" (See chapter 8, "Jungleselling.") The corporate culture at MSA already nurtured creativity, crazy ideas, and fringe notions. But people had to have the courage to feel comfortable in taking part.

Goal-mindedness

Tigers in the bush can run alongside a herd of frantic prey and never once take their eyes off the solitary target they had initially picked out. That was the sort of focus we wanted people to have—and then we'd give them great latitude in how they got there. We had learned the value of that ability to focus on a goal during the bankruptcy days, when there was so much distracting chaos going on all around us. Now some of the goals were changing, but that characteristic was as indispensable as ever.

Versatility

In football, they call it finding "athletes"—that is, men who have the skills and instincts to play a variety of positions. In business, we wanted people who could move from, for example, selling to managing to marketing to communicating to support to any other hat required to stay after the prey.

Empathy

One thing common in people who are good at relationships is empathy. They can spend a few minutes with someone and mine from them what is truly important to them. Then they can respond with information, ideas, and solutions that appeal directly to their perception of the problems.

What we also knew in this eccentric hiring process was that, to the extent we succeeded in finding these tigers, we could never put a leash on them. Their constitutional makeup was such that they would flourish if turned loose, but would die in a pen. It was true then and still is today.

If you make the commitment to track them down, you have to make the commitment to set them free.

FINDING TIGERS THROUGH THE JUNGLE INTERVIEW

Ken Millen was MSA's vice president of human (and animal) resources, and thus the chief bwana on the tiger hunt. When the company began growing, it was his grueling interview program that left some candidates saying the Spanish Inquisition had nothing on the MSA Interview.

For positions of even moderate importance, Millen guided prospective employees on a marathon endurance run that usually entailed a month of time, two to three visits to the company headquarters in Atlanta, and fifteen interviews.

Because tenacity was one of our principal objectives, the process itself was a kind of test. "If after a few visits they said, 'I'm going to hang in there. You're not going to wear me out,' " says Millen, "then we thought we just might have the person we needed."

The interviews, even when we had reached more than 3,000 employees, always included Bill Graves, Ken, other senior managers, the immediate supervisors and managers, the applicant's peers in the company, and myself. We had to have unanimity in the vote. If even one of the fifteen had bad vibrations, the applicant could be vetoed.

Ken Millen:

The value of the process was being able to see people in a lot of different lights, from a lot of different views. Did they want to join the company enough to keep coming back? Would they stick it out?

We were looking for top-notch talent. We would look later for where they would fit into the company in a job sense. We wanted people who had high potential, who could do a lot of things. We would look for entrepreneurial traits. We would look to see if they were truly driven to be successful, if they wanted to compete and win.

75

It was disorganized in many senses. We didn't have a profile that said what degree you should have, what background experience. It was more oriented toward whether this person could run with this competitive group.

One problem we had arose when we began hiring off college campuses. It was a little harder to divine whether some of the applicants had these qualities we sought since they'd spent their lives in academia. Then we hit on the idea of finding out who had gotten dirty in the real world *while* they had been in school.

We began looking for the self-starters, the campus entrepreneurs, the street fighters, the people who had to some extent scraped by in college by holding two or three jobs while going to class, and who solved problems with their wits. These were, for us, more important factors than were their majors, their minors, or their GPAs.

It was not that we disregarded formal education. It takes great discipline and intelligence to get a meaningful diploma, and those qualities have to be considered—although I note that two-thirds of the CEOs of *Fortune* 500 companies were average students. But the traits we found possessed by business tigers just weren't part of any school's curriculum. The vast majority of MSA's people had college degrees, but they also had the scars of initiative.

In the end, we put emphasis on what their genes, their environment, and their experiences had given them, and looked last at what their professors had taught them. Faced with a choice between the erudite pontifications of a Phi Beta Kappa on the future of salesmanship and the insight of a salesperson who'd been in the field for a few years, I know whose advice I would take. And whom I would hire.

At the end of the interview, the tigers' stripes always showed. And the process proved itself over the long run. From it came the tigers we wanted, and they continued performing like those in the original group. The unanimous signoff of applicants proved to ensure the chemistry was right, giving us a low turnover rate of under 15 percent in an industry that hovered around 25 percent.

With the importance MSA put on long-term relationships, hiring people that everyone was comfortable with was critical. If people could connect with fifteen different individuals—from management to technicians to peers—it was clear they understood the rudiments of relationships. And most of them went on to prosper. Apparently, if you could survive the interview, surviving the company was a piece of cake.

MASTERING THE ACID TESTS OF HIRING

Bill Graves, who was second in command at MSA until 1988, could be one of the great intimidators for prospective employees. Greeting this six-foot-seven, 300-pound man was like looking up from the foot of Mount Everest. With hands like catchers' mitts, a somewhat guarded demeanor, and an excruciating propensity for orderly thinking, Graves could be a gauntlet no one wanted to run.

Yet this was the creature who devised what he called the "beer drinking" test. No, not in the chug-a-lug fraternity sense. It was purely an instinctive feeling he was looking for. "If after talking with a prospective employee I didn't feel like going out and having a beer with him and talking some more, I wouldn't hire him," he says. And he wouldn't. He was in search of what he called "the sterling silver person"—people who had it all, the must-hires—and was great at sniffing them out.

Acid tests are a part of any hiring process, and the tests should be determined by the types of people you're seeking. The sheer duration of MSA's interview process—thirty days—was one test that revealed an applicant's determination. The "beer drinking" test told a lot about their ability to connect with a formidable figure who wasn't going to make the interview easy for them.

We brought everyone in to interview with senior management to see how comfortably they interacted with top executives. The reason was twofold: one, we sincerely wanted to meet them; and two, because our sales tactics were from the top down instead of the bottom up, we'd have them pursuing top executives from day one if they were hired. That takes a different mentality than someone who was used to making their case to, for example, whoever answered the door.

Another acid test was their educational environment. MSA had the good fortune to be established just up Peachtree Street from Georgia Tech, which is a kind of farm system for tigers. As a Tech alumnus, I knew that the school was a survival course. It was so ferociously challenging in both academics and problem solving that most of its students could not help but graduate magna cum laude in street fighting.

I know every CEO has a preferred college or two, often their old schools. And I'm sure there are others like Tech that produce great tiger cubs. I won't tell you which institutions' graduates you should avoid, but I will tell you the people to avoid.

At the top of the list is The Talker. This is the person who can expound forever, in minute detail and with oral footnotes, using hot passion and cool logic, about anything. Anything at all. When you check into it, you often find that talking is what they did in school and ever since.

Contrast this with The Doer. This is the person who might not have a résumé in order because he was too busy actually doing things to write one. Between classes, not out of necessity but out of drive, he was in the trenches, earning stripes.

In truth, whether someone is a Talker or a Doer may be determined by genetics and, to a lesser extent, environment. Whether it was a dominant or recessive trait among Georgia Tech's student body, the fact remains that the school could bring out the Doer. Many of MSA's acid tests were geared toward finding out which camp an applicant fell into.

Sometimes there is a tendency to get educationally snobbish in hiring—to look for people who have a specific degree from a specific institution with a specific GPA. That's all okay if they've also shown they can step from the lectern and mix it up on the street. Bill Gates, the chairman of Microsoft Corporation, dropped out of Harvard because he couldn't wait to mix it up. Today, the company he started on a shoestring in 1976 is worth more than IBM.

Of course, integrity is high on the list for tigers. It is harder to gain insight into someone's integrity in a job interview than, for instance, into their technical competence. Sometimes it comes down to an exhaustive background check, other times to your instincts. But finding it in the people you surround yourself with is vital.

Once when I was with Honeywell, my old friend and college professor Pete Jensen was doing some consulting work on computers for a company called Information Systems. He was heading up a large procurement project and, notwithstanding our friendship, Honeywell hadn't been able to get the business from him. A young salesman who reported to me said, "Let's test him."

Pete Jensen:

There's a lot of give and take in these procurements, and I'd set up a lot of benchmarks with which we would evaluate the competition. Honeywell fell short in this very competitive, multimillion-dollar project. When we began to get into the closing steps, I got a call one evening from this Honeywell rep, and I told him the situation. He said, "Well, I understand, but how can I get the business?" I explained again what he was going to have to demonstrate. He came back with, "Yeah, but how can I get the business?"

This was fairly late in the evening, and we talked a few more minutes, and he asked again, "How can I get the business?" I took a deep breath about that time. Then I heard somebody laugh in the background. It was John. The young guy was reporting to him as a salesman. He'd wanted to throw me a fish and see if I'd bite. John just laughed out loud and said, "Pete, I told the bastard it wouldn't work!"

There are a lot of ways to divine someone's character and integrity. The important thing is to do it. The people who play a great game—including the integrity game—should always get the nod over people who talk one.

JUNGLE RULE SUMMARY

NEVER HUNT FOR TIGERS JUST TO PUT THEM ON A LEASH.

Forget the conventional criteria. Look for tenacity, energy, competitiveness, imagination, durability, courage, goal-mindedness, versatility, and empathy.

FINDING TIGERS THROUGH THE JUNGLE INTERVIEW

Your interview process should be a test in itself.

MASTERING THE ACID TESTS OF HIRING

It's not about trick questions, but revealing answers.

7

Jungle Rule #7:
Where the jungle is darkest, use humor as
the light.

Humor. One of the great management tools of the twentieth century. In MSA's race to succeed in the years after bankruptcy, I don't know if anything was more important for us than cultivating an ability to laugh in both good times and bad.

The primary reason I use humor is to make a point. That's the essential thing about humor—its value as a *teaching* device. People tend to remember stories that are couched in a joke. Everyone recalls Clara Peller's "Where's the beef?" for Wendy's. But who remembers what other fast food outlets were doing in their ads ten years ago? Humor endures.

Humor also is a great device to sell, to communicate, and to lessen tensions. It can be used to market products and to liberate creativity. It can help develop relationships with employees, customers, and just about anyone else. It improves interaction among its practitioners. And according to some studies, it even increases wellness and prolongs life. Humor should be indispensable in the corporate culture. Which is why it's a mystery as to why it's so often overlooked—and often even discouraged.

"But wait," you say, "I'm no comic. I hate making speeches, much less trying to be funny." Well, relax. I'm not a comic either. You don't have to be a comic to enjoy the benefits of humor. You don't even have to be funny. You just have to have a "sense" of humor—you need only enjoy it, understand it, appreciate it, and cultivate it.

If you do that, whatever points you make to people—and business persons make a lot of them—will have much longer lives. Humor leaves people talking about the lesson, repeating the lesson, reliving the lesson, and thus better learning the lesson. And they remember the source.

Having said that, I'll also say that I don't advise humor for everybody. Some individuals just can't bring it off. Others are fine in private, but freeze up in public. Still others, perhaps intimidated, haven't tested the water. (Robin Williams was a late bloomer; he says he never said anything funny in his life until he tried to pick up girls in college.)

Don't try to be something besides yourself. Amplify and project your own personality. The point I want to make in this chapter is that if humor is there for you, use it. The benefits are awesome.

The payoff on humor is that you, your message, and your company get remembered. And those are the goals of all business communication. You get ready access to minds because people are eager to hear good stories. Your advertising is rarely overlooked. Salespersons are seldom ignored. Conferences are enthusiastically attended.

People love a show. If they can learn something in the process, mission accomplished.

IF YOU CAN TALK, YOU CAN SPEAK

When I first began public speaking, I wasn't funny. I mumbled. I was self-conscious. I was nervous. I stuttered. I did a lot wrong. I got criticized so much for making poor presentations, that, in order to be a professional in this business, I just consciously began to work at it.

My personality was always outgoing (a gift from my mother, who never forgets a name or a story). I loved to laugh. I picked up on stories easily and could tell them pretty well in conversation. Meanwhile, as I experimented, trying to emulate others I'd heard speak, I realized I wasn't doing what was easy for me to do.

To be at ease speaking, I learned, you just do what you do in a conversation—except you have the conversation with a hundred or two hundred or ten thousand people. I never hide behind a podium. I always use a lavalier microphone and walk around, make eye contact with lots of people, and converse. Along the way, I use humor to make my points.

If you use humor, you've got to be willing to try things. You don't really need the courage of a tiger, but sometimes you need the hide of one. You have to live down the murmurs after a bombed joke—and not panic in the eerie silence of a tough audience. Once, Dick Cavett, after going through his entire stand-up routine at a nightclub early in his career, had heard not a solitary laugh from his audience. When he closed, he said, "I'd like to thank you for coming out tonight. And I'd like to congratulate you all on looking remarkably lifelike." Well, the bartender laughed.

If I get one of Cavett's audiences—and it has happened—I possess a luxury he didn't: I can deliver my talk straight. So can you. But the prospect of an occasional tough audience shouldn't intimidate you from using humor to communicate.

There are four types of people, and three of them don't use humor: (1) people who can use it and do; (2) people who can't use it and don't; (3) people who can use it, but don't, and (4) people who can't use it, but do anyway. Most people who fall into (3) are there

83

because they have agonized through speeches by (4). They shouldn't let the experience turn them off to humor as a corporate resource.

More people can use humor than believe they can, so test yourself. And even if you're not one of them, you still can breed humor as part of your corporate culture by encouraging others to use it.

Among many other things, the reward is more acute imagination in the company. Humor allows people the freedom of fantasy. It allows them to approach the extremes, even the absurd. The most exciting creativity is found on the fringes. Humor might be the most liberating of all Jungle Rule themes. As for reaching people, humor is one of the most common of human denominators, just behind hunger and just ahead of sex.

To build that culture, you have to be able to laugh at yourself—in public. Level the playing field. Remove the pretensions and pomp and circumstance that people hang around your neck. I've probably given about two thousand speeches in my career, most of them as CEO. Often the persons introducing a CEO will want to build up the person to solemn sainthood. I always jump off that pedestal with a joke.

One of my favorites is "Fatty the Chairman." It has gotten a lot of audiences on my side over the years—even resistant ones. The world has some notoriously tough audiences for humor. For Americans, any English audience can be intimidating. The English are wonderful people, but they have a reputation for laughing only at Anglo-centric humor—Englishmen and English jokes about English events and English culture.

I once spoke in London and was introduced as "a great technologist," one of many things I'm not. So I did my schtick and all these technical people in the audience were looking at each other, asking, "Who is this guy?" Nobody laughed. I tried things in the middle of the speech. Nothing worked. I'd lost them. Their expectations had been fixed on hearing from "a great technologist," and I'd let them down. Next time, I would rearrange expectations.

Then some time later, I had the great honor of speaking at Royal Albert Hall in London to about four thousand managing directors from throughout Britain. I was among many luminaries, including business leaders, British lords and ladies, ministers of parliament, as well as Prince Charles. The fellow who introduced me laid on all the good stuff. "John Imlay has been called 'One of the Fifteen People Most Likely to Influence Computing in the Next Five Years.' " He even mentioned my selection as "America's Best-Dressed Businessman."

I wanted to get the audience to identify with me as just a businessman, a regular fellow, so I started off with the story that has done that for me many times:

> *The other day I came into our office here [in London] and my car was missing and sputtering. I pulled into the carpark, forgetting how big our company had gotten. I was fuming and fussing the way you do when your car is broken down. So I picked up the phone and called old Harry down in administration. I said, "Harry, my car is broken. I need to borrow the estate wagon."*
>
> *He said, "John, I'm now a senior vice president. I don't handle that anymore."*
>
> *"But what do I do?" I asked. He said, "Dial 3198." So dutifully, I dial 3198. A very enthusiastic young voice answers. "Motor Pool."*
>
> *"Motor Pool?" I said. "What have you got down there?" He says, "We've got lorries for going back and forth to the factory. We've got estate wagons to pick up folks at the airport. We've got Oldsmobiles and Pontiacs for the vice presidents. We've got a big, old Cadillac for our big, old president. And we've got a Mercedes for Fatty, our chairman."*
>
> *I said, "Do you know who this is!" He said, "No."*
> *I said, "This is John Imlay—your chairman." Long pause.*
> *Finally he said, "Do you know who this is?"*
> *I said, "No."*
> *He said, "So long, Fatty."*

The point of recounting the joke for you is to demonstrate that humor doesn't have to be a series of snappy one-liners. I use humor simply to make my points. Those points usually can't even be made with one-liners. They are better served with anecdotes. It's the sometimes crazy metaphor within the anecdote, the dramatic or bizarre imagery, that helps people understand the point you're trying to convey. And it is the humor that makes the anecdote memorable—and repeatable.

In the case of "Fatty the Chairman," I've taught the audience that I'm not all wrapped up in self-image, that I laugh at myself and they can laugh, too, that they can relax while they listen. It instantly changes the mood of the audience.

The corporate personality is something that is largely reflected in advertising and other public images. If a CEO leads the way to humor, it will show up in the media messages people create about the company—and in the way people remember the company.

"HA! I LAUGH IN THE FACE OF DANGER!"

Remember the old swashbuckler movies when the valiant swordsman would be facing almost certain death at the hands of the evil horde, then would smile cannily and utter those words? It might have seemed corny, but it was great management theory.

While working our way through bankruptcy, we found that humor lightened the depressing blackness of the situation. It got people's attention when they might have been thinking about writing résumés or taking up yoga. That was important, because, now that we were racing ahead with the company, we had a lot of optimistic beliefs to pass on. But we needed to get through that crust of doubt and fear. We needed all of their attention. Humor delivered it.

It went beyond employees. I once gave a speech in Denver before ADAPSO, the software industry trade association. I was trying, in the speech, to illustrate how software companies and the industry in general were changing, were moving from services to products, were troubled but had a robust future.

At the time, I was a young nonentity trying to make a serious impression on the industry's movers and leave them with a positive image of MSA. I could have taken the serious, pedantic route inasmuch as I was talking about a serious subject (bankruptcy and rebirth). But I took a chance and used the nine lives of the "Bankruptcy Ain't So Bad" presentation and *Gone With the Wind* visuals I had given to employees.

I wanted to get away from the talking head, so I used the visuals to add color and drama to the speech. The humor had gotten them to look and to listen, and the visuals made the message easy to understand.

There were probably three dozen visual metaphors in that classic movie that I tied to MSA's growth, collapse, tribulations, and resurrection. The presentation went over so well that I showed it to user group meetings. I didn't want to deceive anyone that we were in bankruptcy; but I found I could greatly alleviate their fears by laying out our plans in interesting and funny ways.

Even amid all of the changes the company has seen, the humor in the MSA culture has remained intact throughout its life—and, in doing so, kept other things intact. Once it has a life of its own, it will help you through trauma or change or darkness. It is one corporate asset that never depreciates. Humor gives strength as well as laughs. It can lighten you and enlighten you. And it can unite you. An amazing thing, a laugh.

IF YOU JUGGLE SACRED COWS, EVENTUALLY ONE WILL LAND ON YOU

Humor has its payoff, but it also has its price. That price is apt to go up a little in this edgy world of political correctness, where it sometimes seems that no one is allowed to laugh. Even innocent humor can sometimes slay a sacred cow you never would suspect was in the audience.

In the speech at Royal Albert Hall, I used a slide with the initials "IBM" on it to talk about the future of computing. IBM, a company I respect a lot, had always pushed huge mainframe computers as business's solution to computing problems, but there was evidence the world wanted smaller computers. The next slide I put up said IBM stood for "I've Been Misled." The crowd loved it.

The next day John Akers, the chairman of IBM back then, sent four guys down to tell me to take the slide out because it injured IBM. They didn't like the decibel level of the laugh I got. I told them, "Look at this video of my presentation and see if it 'injures' IBM." They watched and said, no, it didn't, and went back to tell Akers. Still, the head of IBM England, who had heard the speech, went away unhappy.

I once told a story about the ultimate computer that would be built on the moon in the year 2000. It would have all the answers and would connect with every machine in the world. At the designated moment, the president throws the switch and every computer worldwide blinks. The first question put to the machine is: Is there a God? The answer comes back: There is now.

For this indiscretion, I received a weighty, single-spaced letter that began, "You are a blasphemer!" That was followed by sixteen pages of parables.

I wrote back a letter of apology.

Even if you believe you're the most customer-oriented person ever—as I do—humor can put you at sword's point with some astute fencers. I once was speaking at a conference of chief information officers at Laguna Beach, California. I was doing a "What's In–What's Out" list. "Democracy is in, Noriega is out!" On the list I had, "Ninja Turtles are in, Ken and Barbie are out!"

This did not go over well with John Phippen, the CIO of Mattel—which manufactures Ken and Barbie—who was an extremely important client sitting smack in the middle of the audience. He left fuming, then later shot us through the heart with a letter saying Barbie sales *alone* were greater than the entire value of my company, accounting for $1.1 billion of Mattel's $2 billion in revenue.

The reality of humor is that you get so close to boundaries and images and metaphors that you will inevitably cross the line. There are risks. You are going to offend somebody, sometimes completely innocently, and they will tell you about it in unambiguous ways. An angry environmentalist might kill three trees to get the paper to condemn a joke about tree killing. But it is all part of the business of humor.

My advice is simple: Don't do anything blue or blatant or mean-spirited that is likely to offend your audience or your customers. But don't curtail your creativity because of the fear of isolated outbursts. Two thousand speeches and fifty thousand jokes later, I can tell you the rewards of humor are worth indulging the occasional tirade. And sometimes you can even get a joke out of those.

JUNGLE RULE SUMMARY

WHERE THE JUNGLE IS DARKEST, USE HUMOR AS THE LIGHT.

Humor is a wondrous teaching device in both good times and bad.

IF YOU CAN TALK, YOU CAN SPEAK

You don't have to be a golden-throated orator to communicate, or a comedian to use humor.

"HA! I LAUGH IN THE FACE OF DANGER!"

Humor can revitalize people even during traumas.

IF YOU JUGGLE SACRED COWS, EVENTUALLY ONE WILL LAND ON YOU

The rewards of using humor far outweigh the fallout from the unintended offense.

8

JUNGLESELLING

Jungle Rule #8:
Sell it in the treetops.

So you're in sales and the streets are mean. The leads are cold enough to have wind chill factors. Your commission plan has been "reformulated" again. The kids need school clothes, the anniversary approaches, and assistant manager trainees are slamming the door on your eager toe when you try to wedge it in. Is this what's getting you down? Well, cheer up. You've just been beating the jungle's paths when you should have been working the treetops.

The leanest, quickest, most effective way to sell is at the top of the organization. Decisions are made faster, with less politics and fewer amendments, and the sale is more likely to stick because there are fewer higher-ups to overrule it. If there is a grand lesson in my thirty-five years of selling, it is: *aim high.*

But in the sometimes hardscrabble business of sales, far too many salespersons still get caught up in the notion of "getting a toe in the door" at some low or intermediate level in the company. That's called bottom-up selling and it's a long road to the top with no guarantees.

This isn't an argument for you to circumvent bona fide decision makers, because that's a sure path to alienation. But the relationship to cultivate, and the person to aim for, is the top decision maker. Once you know who that is, use your knowledge, your contacts, and your imagination to meet them. And it doesn't matter how high up they are.

Selling in the treetops was a concept we pushed at MSA from the day we took over. From the days of bankruptcy through the company's rise to $250 million in sales, the strategy never changed—and, in fact, was a major reason for our success. The idea was one I acquired before I ever joined MSA.

When I was selling computers for Honeywell, a big contract with the state of Georgia was one of my targets. It was a contract that IBM had kept a lock on for years by avoiding competitive bids, a practice I thought it was time to end.

I'd been trying to distinguish myself with customers back in those days by riding around with them in my Cadillac and just having some fun. The problem was, they weren't the right customers. My boss at Honeywell chewed me out for spending too much time and energy on the wrong audience.

"You deal with all these low levels," he said. "They all love you. You're 'King of the Hot Dogs,' but you're never at the top." I sulked for a while, especially about getting beaten by the IBM salesman in the government deal. Then I decided to take the message seriously.

In the upcoming gubernatorial election, the contract was up to sell again. Everyone was positive that Bo Calloway, a Republican, would win against Democrat Lester Maddox. I worked on Calloway's campaign—goal sharing—because I agreed with him and his election was a certainty. Calloway would then be the final decision maker for this multimillion-dollar deal.

But then a third-party candidate entered the election and snatched 8 percent of the vote. Calloway got more votes than Maddox, but was just short of a 50 percent majority, so the election went to the Georgia legislature, which was controlled by Democrats. They promptly concluded that Maddox was the man the people really wanted, votes aside, and made him governor. Honeywell and I were out, IBM was in. Again.

Still alive, however, was my determination to sell this at the top. The players had changed, but the strategy was the same. The questions were how to meet Maddox and what to say to him.

Maddox himself provided the opportunity to meet with him. Once a month he held court in a foyer at the Governor's Mansion during what the press called "Little People's Day." It was an event where just regular folks could line up and spend a few minutes venting their frustrations personally to the governor.

Maddox in a way also provided me with the ammunition to sway him. He was, as history shows, a man of great passions and prejudices. One of those passions was a furious hatred of communism. Another was a grim dislike for the Kennedys.

On Little People's Day, I got in line at 9 A.M. with a fold-out bulletin board I'd made that contained the whole story I thought Maddox should hear. When I reached him I opened the bulletin board. There was a headline from *The Augusta Courier* that read: "IBM Sells to the Communists." Another read: "IBM Gets Contract with No Bid."

"Governor," I said, "I went to Georgia Tech and I'm a salesman for Honeywell. You need to know right off that IBM comes in here without competitive bids and gets all the state's business. Meanwhile, this is what they do," and I showed him photographs of the Kennedys and IBM chairman Tom Watson, Jr., sailing happily together aboard a yacht.

Maddox said, "Give me your card. I want to see you personally." A few days later I got a call from his assistant, inviting me to a private conversation with Maddox. It was an interesting experience, to say the least. He had a mynah bird and, while Maddox played the piano, the bird and I sang "Peg O' My Heart." At the end of the meeting, he said, "We're gonna blow this noncompetition thing wide open." He threw out IBM and I sold him six Honeywell mainframe computers.

The lesson was clear and served as the foundation for MSA's sales strategies for two decades: *sell at the top*. Without question, the best leads are the ones that identify decision makers, not role players. Once you know who they are, find out what motivates them, what their passions and goals are, then find a forum in which to meet them personally.

If you end up being rejected, it's a rejection you would have had anyway, except after a much longer process. But always ask for the business only from those who can give it to you. As they say in the jungle, you don't ask the squirrel if you can eat the lion's kill.

APPEAL TO THE *SEMPER FIDELIS*

One of the best by-products of selling at the top is that you tend to get people who are, to borrow the U.S. Marines' theme, *semper fidelis*—ever faithful. They may have other names within the company—"angels" and "foxes" were popular at MSA—but they all do the same thing. For many reasons, they can make a sale stick. They make it stick with financial resources and human resources that other people simply don't have at their disposal. They can use persuasion, motivation, or commands. The dynamic is simply that the higher up a decision is made, the more difficult it is for someone farther down the ladder to overturn it. You also get more support from more people in the company because they tend to follow the leader.

The *semper fi* person becomes the product champion, just by the power of his office and the force of his conviction. The result of all this is a longer faithfulness to your products—certainly long enough for you to prove the decision was a wise one. (Warning: The downside of going to the *semper fi* decision maker is that if your product bombs that first time, your second chance will come when hell freezes over.)

As a young salesman, I had a shot at a mammoth sale at Fort Benning, Georgia. It was for an armaments tracking and accounting system that would comprise seven machines dubbed Univac 1004s, which were actually excellent systems. The top decision maker in this project was a Colonel Skruggs.

Colonel Skruggs had been *semper fidelis* to IBM for years. You almost expected him to salute when he spoke the company's name. So it wasn't easy to hit him with the truth.

"You're making a huge mistake," I told him, which was accurate. "We have one machine—the 1004—that can do twenty times what IBM's machine can do, and for less money."

He would spring to his feet and defend IBM with great passion. I decided he needed to see the 1004 in action and then sell himself before he could ever champion the product in his unit. One way or another, I absolutely had to get that wonderful, blind loyalty over to my side.

I flew him to Univac headquarters in Blue Bell, Pennsylvania, for a demonstration that would show unarguably that the 1004 was a vastly superior machine. But the demonstration I set up wasn't just to show off its accounting functions. To get his loyalty, I needed to show him a computer that would be loyal in the field. Unlike the IBM machines of the day, the 1004 was tough, portable, and didn't require air-conditioning—perfect, it turned out, for military activity in rough, steamy theaters such as Southeast Asia, which at the time America was being drawn into. Colonel Skruggs had found new loyalty.

He ordered seven 1004s. And now that he had this loyalty, he wouldn't countenance any disloyalty from subordinates, which is great for a salesperson. The colonel called a meeting to announce his fidelity. He paced up and down, slapping a riding crop against his thigh.

"We're committed to this Univac 1004," he announced sternly. "This is the greatest machine in history. It will be the liaison for parts as we go to war."

One guy sitting in the back looked horrified. "I ran one of those 1004s once, Colonel. It gave me an electrical shock!"

"Then *you* will be the operator," the Colonel informed him, much to his dismay. "Next question!"

There were no more questions. Only *semper fidelis*.

LEARN YOUR SECRET ASSETS

Let's talk secret weapons.

One advantage of making people the centerpiece of your business is that they are infinitely more versatile than our cleverest gadgets. People can interact, interpret, and respond, all of which relationships require. But it is the number of levels on which they can do this that really build common bonds with people, customers or otherwise. It is certainly useful in sales.

Relationships can be eccentric things in the selling business, which incidentally everyone in a company—from receptionist to technician to salesperson to CEO—happens to be in. It is only the *transaction* that is between the salesperson and customer.

But the special intimacies surrounding the transaction might account for why most of the eccentricities show up among the parties involved in it. And it's why people in sales should recognize that, in the right circumstances, *anything* about them can be an asset, no matter how distant it might be from any other tool they ever used to close a sale. Or whether they ever will use it again. Most people probably have a hundred hidden assets they can use, but often don't know it.

Obviously, as we've discussed, important assets come in whatever ideas, tools, and means you have to help a customer accomplish his or her goals. Maybe that would be your technical skill (or technical resources), your business knowledge, your contacts, your experiences.

Sometimes these assets are on another level not necessarily related to goal sharing, but to building your relationships through common ground.

They come in the forms of specialized knowledge (sports, politics, cars, movie trivia, literature, travel, crafts, fitness, the environment—anything that has been interesting enough for you to become conversant in it); skills (art, writing, crafts, woodworking, athletic competition, etc.); allegiances (to teams, businesses, colleges, causes, etc.). Anything that might provide common ground for discourse and exploration. It is always surprising to find out how much more you have in common with people than superficial conversations reveal. So never let your conversations be superficial.

In relationships, it's important to share goals, views, and plans to get that vital synergy going. But it's also important, especially for sellers, to share some of the customer's passions. Even the offbeat ones. That's usually when your "hidden assets" get sent into the game.

E. W. "Mac" McCain, one of my most treasured mentors, once gave me a lesson in exploiting hidden assets. As soon as I met him, I saw instantly that he not only was smart, but was a master at getting close to people. He'd graduated with honors from the Citadel, where he'd taken a degree in accounting and earned a prestigious scholarship (which he declined for family reasons) to the Wharton School of Finance for his master's. Impressive stuff, but it was Mac's collegiate sport—wrestling—that he called upon to help close a sale we were working on.

We were trying to land an account with the U.S. Marines for a quartermaster inventory system. Our system was good, but it wasn't substantially different from the competition's. That's when you look for the personal edge. We had been working the treetops to find the top guy, who turned out to be General William Battel. The general liked our ideas and enthusiasm, which led him to agree to the purchase.

About that time, however, the conversation turned to wrestling, a passion of the general's. The conversation between Mac and the general got pretty animated. Finally the Warrior General said, "I'll take you on."

The Warrior Salesman stood and replied, "Let's go."

To the surprise, and maybe horror, of everyone around, the two of them stripped down to their shorts and went at it. As I watched them out there, sweating and pounding each other with an effort matched only by their joy, I had this horrible vision that Mac might hammerlock us out of a sale. The pride of a wrestler was bad enough, I thought, but could a *wrestling Marine* stand defeat?

"Mac!" I called to him from the sidelines. "We got the order!"

And we kept it. Mac didn't throw the match (unthinkable), which was even. And General Battel was exultant afterward, just for the joy of momentary combat. He happily signed for the order. It was a great lesson about getting close to people (literally and figuratively, in this case) through passions. It showed me that buying is emotional. And your sales tools—a double leg drop, a headlock, etc.—aren't always what they showed you in sales training. And that, if your product is the same as the competition's, the difference is you.

IMLAY'S QUICK GUIDE TO EXPLOITING YOUR HIDDEN ASSETS

Ask questions!

A lot of relationships either don't materialize or begin to deteriorate because people stop asking questions. We think we know everything about someone, or at least enough to get by, that there are no more mysteries, no more dimensions to explore. Our interest wanes and so does the relationship.

The truth is, most people are like icebergs: much lies below the surface. In business, you need to *ask* questions, *listen* to answers, and *think* like a detective.

Listen for ways to share goals.

You always do what you can to help people attain their business goals. It might be as simple as a successful installation of your product. It might be as complex as figuring out how to make a company profitable. But just the exercise of actively thinking about solving problems this way does three fundamental things: It often helps the person; it makes you a more effective problem solver in the future; and it dramatically energizes the relationship. Make the customer's goal your common ground, and they usually will do the same for yours.

Follow the passions.

Business goals aren't the only common ground. Most people are slaves to their passions. They like to talk about them, cheer for them, rant against them, and play them out. General Battel's penchant for wrestling is one example. Other people are passionate about politics, sports, technology, automobiles, fitness, their children, and a thousand other things. Without sounding nosy, ask the questions that ferret out these passions. If it's something you are well versed in, get the conversation going. If it's something you're not, invite them to tell you about it.

Do your homework.

Mac's wrestling match with General Battel was a spontaneous use of a hidden asset, but a little research can help you prepare to engage someone's passions. Does he have season tickets to a given team's games? Has she recently won an award for humanitarian activity? Did he recently publish a paper or write a book? Once you have some insight into their interests, you can study up on them enough to talk—or at least listen—intelligently. But your interest must always be sincere, not artificial.

Use your other relationships.

Often you will be able to match up someone's passions with a relationship you already have. It doesn't cost a fortune and it's fun.

Sports is one good example. I'm an avid golfer, and golf is as close to a common denominator as there is among businesspersons. When I can, I arrange for a round with other players who will make it a special day for my guest. I stay active in Atlanta golf and athletic clubs, so I maintain relationships with a lot of good players, including celebrities.

Dun & Bradstreet Software can put you in the front row behind the backstop for Atlanta Braves contests and in a skybox for Atlanta Falcons football. Too conventional? When someone has indicated an interest, we've treated them to mud wrestling. And if someone likes the theater, we can do the impossible and find seats for *Phantom of the Opera* on Broadway the day of the show.

Who do you know who could give your budding relationship an unexpectedly personal touch? If you've taken the time to cultivate relationships, you'll find you have a lot of friends ready to help you cultivate even more of them.

Don't waste their time.

The process of exploring goals, passions, and relationships sometimes turns up subjects that people pointedly don't want to talk about. You never should press a sore subject, such as a recent divorce or a family tragedy. And even in the process of creating a relationship environment in which you are selling to friends, you can wear out your welcome by trying too hard. You just have to be completely natural in your conversations, not pushy or obsessive or nosy. And you must *always* respect the fact that their time is valuable.

Deliver on your business promise.

Don't forget that a business commitment—colloquially referred to as a "sale"—is what began your relationship. That may also be what constitutes 90 percent of the relationship, even if you get to be friends. The message is simple: Do at least what you said you would do; and when you can, do more.

"WHERE DO I SIGN, MR. PRESIDENT?"

One of the fun things about jungleselling is imagining ways to get people to help you. I've always believed that everyone in a company—certainly every tiger—is in sales in one way or another. Clearly, everyone is selling the company when they meet people on the outside. Developers are selling the products by the excellence they put into them. Receptionists and switchboard personnel sell first impressions and efficiency. Support people sell a company's commitment to The Promise. Tigers in a group are called a family, and selling, ideally, should be a family affair.

If you're imaginative enough, though, you can even get your

extended family involved in jungleselling. Sometimes I would have Fran Tarkenton, whose office was nearby, sit in on a closing, dispensing autographed footballs and playing-field war stories. People loved it. As already mentioned, during our bankruptcy proceedings we made a point of getting the court's imprimatur on every contract. It was a source of great comfort for customers who viewed it as a federal guarantee that the software was good. I've personally sat in on thousands of closings over the years, talking to customers about our products, our strategies, whatever was on their minds. But the greatest use of extended family came when we worked hand in hand with a former U.S. president to raise funds for a project of his as well as close some business of ours. It was goal sharing at its finest.

We had struck up a friendly relationship with former President Gerald Ford, who had keynoted some of our conferences and been a great hit with his observations, wit, and self-deprecating humor. We'd become close enough friends that he would call me for games of golf, among other things.

One of those other things was for a donation to his Presidential Library, a project extremely important to him. I was perfectly happy to make one, but it occurred to me that President Ford could do both his library and MSA a favor if he was willing to have a little fun.

We had some clients in Michigan, Ford's home state, who were on the fence about buying.

"Mr. President," I said, "I have a proposition for you. If you'll get on the phone and mention a few kind words about MSA, I'll give your library a percentage of all the sales we're able to close. You could end up with a lot more than a regular donation."

To my delight, he agreed to do it.

So here were these data processing managers and financial executives up in Michigan, sitting around the office sipping coffee on a typical workday, when the phone rings and a voice says, "Please hold the line for President Gerald Ford." Right.

Then Ford's unmistakable voice is there. He would chat amiably for a while. There was no blatant solicitation. In essence, he told them that he was doing some fund-raising for his library and that MSA was a significant contributor to the effort. And to whatever extent they could support MSA, they would also be helping the library fund.

Normally, Ford would have received $10,000 for a donation. Instead, he got $38,000 for his library for having a little creative fun. And MSA got $3.8 million.

I can testify that in our experience, former presidents have a 100 percent closure rate in sales.

SWARMSELLING SENDS A SERVICE MESSAGE

One thing we did in the beginning years at MSA—and much more feverishly as we built resources—was swarmselling. It was known by other names as well, including "team selling" and "schoolbus selling." The idea was to make certain a prospective client knew we understood their problem (and the solution) at every level, from the mail room to the executive suites, not just that the software would run on his computer.

So instead of sending one or two sellers to make a presentation—the industry standard—we often took the aggressive tack. We would show up with eight or twelve people, including district managers, top technical staff, and even executive officers.

Rick Page, who headed up sales training for MSA and was in charge of the southeast region for sales, put it this way: "We played hardball. Instead of just selling a project's functionality, we sold executive solutions. In the team-selling approach, everyone knew our products and the competition's products. And they all knew the client's goals. When the client asked for a presentation, we'd in turn ask for their vice presidents to be there. With team selling, we could answer any question anyone asked."

When your central corporate message is that *people are the key,* you have to demonstrate your commitment to it at the first possible opportunity in the marketplace. That usually is the sale, or at least the road to the sale. A lot of companies have similar themes, and some even have pretty fair execution of the concept. But many keep it hidden from view for far too long. They rely on a seller's words instead of the company's actions to convince a prospective customer it exists at all. It's a mistake to wait.

Some companies turn loose their sellers, then instruct them to articulate—as opposed to demonstrate—the theory of commitment to people. They *tell* the prospects they have great support. They *tell* them they have exceptional product strategies. They *tell* them they have visionary management. They *tell* them they can help them succeed.

And they're usually telling them all this while sitting alone at the far end of the table.

Everyone says the same thing. Big deal. Saying it distinguishes you not one iota from the competition. You have to *show* prospects you are exceptional, and you have to show them at the first possible moment. What better place than the sales presentation?

Two things get accomplished when you attack this way. One is that the prospects often are overwhelmed that so many top people are involved from day one. That show of initial support always works in your favor. The second reason is because, by bringing in more top people and asking the prospects to do the same thing, you have a better chance of meeting the *semper fidelis*, the fox, the inside person who will fight for you.

"Our selling focused on solution selling and the hierarchy of the people you were dealing with," says Page. "Not technology or anything else, but how to go in and find the person called the fox. You go in and find the fox and get the fox's support. The fox introduces you to all the players and pushes the order through for you."

If you're doing team selling right, you end up with the fox at the sales presentation, along with everyone the fox might need to influence. Executives answer executives' questions, technicians answer technicians' questions, and so on, and everyone comes away from the meeting singing from the same hymnal. It makes the job easier for the fox, which can facilitate the close.

The next time an important prospect is on the line, don't just send your best seller, send your best team. Then swarm.

PEOPLE AFFECT THE PSYCHOLOGY OF PRICING

There's nothing to business really, somebody once said. All you have to do is sell something for more than it costs you to make it. Simple, right? Except that determining that price is one of the great arcane arts of free enterprise, where all that is free is your right to make a choice. But what to choose?

In the first several years after MSA emerged from bankruptcy, we wanted market share and sold like it. We would deal with anybody. We had a pretty sophisticated grasp of what our profit margins were. And, under the guiding principle of *whatever it takes,* we would cut some pretty attractive deals. But it turned out we were shortchanging ourselves in the most literal way.

The formula we developed for selling our entire company as a support group held a lot more sway with customers, we learned, than if we'd just sold them a software product. The thing we did as a matter of policy—make MSA an extension of the client's company—helped us in the matter of pricing. We still would deal, but we found customers were willing to pay a premium for the certainty of aggressive support. It was extremely interesting psychology.

"There are a lot of bottom-dwellers in this business," says Jeff Fisher, a former MSA sales manager. "They'll sell their software for whatever they can get for it. I remember once we were involved in a tooth-and-nail competition for this hundred-thousand-dollar-plus system. University Computing Company was in it and so was Financial Technology, Inc. All of our bids had been around a hundred and forty thousand dollars. At the last minute, UCC cut its price to seventy thousand dollars. Financial Technology did the same. The bank president had us all in to hear our stories.

" 'What's your best price?' he asked us. The other companies stated theirs. Then he asked me.

" 'You have our best price,' I told him. It was still a hundred and forty thousand. I got the order."

What happened here was a simple realization that more had to be bought in this transaction than a software product. The bank president foresaw too many corners being cut by the other companies that had slashed their prices. They had violated his comfort zone. That laid the deal squarely in MSA's lap.

The lesson was that people put a premium on people, and we liked to believe that people were MSA's strength. To the extent that you can transcend the idea of selling a product and evolve to that of selling your people—the product being a bridge between the two companies—then you've laid the psychological foundation to ask a better price for your wares.

People are the key.

JUNGLE RULE SUMMARY

SELL IT IN THE TREETOPS.

.Don't waste your time getting a toe in the door, unless it's to the chairman's office.

APPEAL TO THE SEMPER FIDELIS

Somewhere in every company is the "fox" who will be ever faithful to you and your product.

LEARN YOUR SECRET ASSETS

A little self-examination will show you dozens of ways to establish common bonds in a relationship.

"WHERE DO I SIGN, MR. PRESIDENT?"

If you're bold enough to ask, you can extend the tiger family to include the biggest cats around.

SWARMSELLING SENDS A SERVICE MESSAGE

The sales presentation is the first opportunity to demonstrate that your corporate commitment to support is more than lip service.

PEOPLE AFFECT THE PSYCHOLOGY OF PRICING

You can be more aggressive in pricing your wares if customers believe they are buying your people and not just your product.

9

THEM THAT DOES, GETS

Jungle Rule #9:
If you capture dinner, you get to eat it.

Edmund Wilson once said, "There is nothing more demoralizing than a small but adequate income."

I agree. That view has left me with a saying on the delicate matter of compensation: "Them that does, gets." Grammar aside, it has served as a pillar of my compensation policies ever since a fellow named Jay Forrester, who was then the president of Univac, bought me breakfast some years back. All he did over eggs that morning was screw my commission ceiling so far down that I had to move my toes to ask for an order. It was a great lesson in how not to treat sellers. I never forgot it.

I was working for Univac at the time. I'd recently sold seven large computers dubbed 1004s to a single customer, an accomplishment that left me with Univac's single-season record for 1004 sales and for commissions—about $210,000 in 1961 dollars. Selling one or two a year was normal, so my seven got a lot of attention from the Univac management. The company decided to send me around the country to meet executives and other salespersons. It was supposed to be a motivational tour of sorts. It failed. When it was over, the only thing I was motivated to do was leave.

I was excited to meet Forrester. I'd anticipated that he wanted to meet the country's top salesman that year, maybe pick my brain for some insights that could be passed along to other salespersons.

"Imlay," he said to start the conversation, "how much money did you make last year?"

Well, I thought, *that's* an icebreaker. "Two hundred and ten thousand dollars," I told him proudly.

His expression didn't really change when he said, "A salesman isn't worth more than fifteen thousand dollars a year. We're paying you too much."

End of conversation. And breakfast.

Forrester, I learned later, was a financial man who rapidly concluded that his income for the prior year had been less than mine. Because he was from finance and not sales, salespersons were little more than anonymous line items to him, not people who made the company successful. And no line item was going to earn $210,000. Forrester was probably an excellent executive on all other counts, but his myopia on sales compensation was his fatal flaw. Here was a guy who, faced with a tiger, thought it best to cut him down to a kitten. That's when tigers leave home.

It wasn't just me. Forrester set about slashing Univac's entire commission structure companywide. I tried to make a go of it, as did other top sellers. But the future was limited when the head of the company had prevalued your services at $15,000. The exodus began. The reason wasn't inferior technology, declining market share, or poor strategic planning. The sole reason was destructively undervalued salespersons. It was at this point that Univac began to fail in its competition against IBM. At least, that's the way I see it.

The problem boiled down to one thing: Forrester had never developed relationships with people in sales. He didn't understand their goals, their egos, their aspirations, or the value they had conferred upon their work. He regarded them as "plug-in" personnel, imminently expendable, even though they were pretty sophisticated individuals selling highly complex technical equipment.

The experience instilled in me the belief that if you're out there successfully prowling the trenches and selling, your value is enormous. It could be argued that I have this perspective because I'm a CEO who came up through sales. Possibly. But from that day, I've insisted that the ceilings on sales compensation be extremely high—just the opposite of the Forrester Plan.

If the right tigers are in place—people who are internally motivated, imaginative, resourceful, and persistent—they will go to the ends of the earth to bring in sale after sale. Success is addictive for them when the rewards don't diminish.

It is an approach that is not without its problems. There are territorial jealousies, client envy, and the feared complacency of "the comfort zone." But dealing with these relatively trivial perils—which incidentally is almost always done from an atmosphere of super-high performance—is infinitely more productive than the reverse. Fighting the fires of stunted morale, bitterness toward management, and perpetual turnover are battles always fought in poorly performing environments. I say, let the successful succeed. If they're bringing it in, let them take it home.

MAKE COMPENSATION A LIFESTYLE, NOT A PAYCHECK

A nice paycheck is only one tier in the arena of compensation. We always believed at MSA that compensation was multifaceted. We tried to take the idea of compensation from a semimonthly event to a kind of lifestyle. You've heard people talk about working in a "rewarding environment," and that's what we sought. But what is it?

Clearly it begins with a company that takes the time to understand its employees, help them set goals, figure out ways to share those goals, pay them well, challenge them, excite them, believe in them, and arm them with the tools to do their jobs. To the extent you're in tune with the goals of those people around you, and are actively working to help them achieve those goals, that's a form of compensation. It's part of the *environment.* You're helping them to advance in life, which is something a paycheck doesn't do, though people often believe otherwise.

But whenever you survey people and ask them the top ten things that motivate them, money usually comes in somewhere between fifth and seventh. What's always nearer the top are recognition and peer respect.

Norman Mailer once wrote that ego is "the Great Word of the Twentieth Century." He was right. Sometimes ego gets a bad rap because it has some ugly manifestations. But I'm not turned off by the word. In truth we should celebrate ego. It is ego that drives people to be the rainmakers, the doers, the achievers. A paycheck only goes part of the way toward ego satisfaction. There are three other "P's" that should come into play:

Prominence

One simple way to stroke an ego is recognition. At MSA, we created clubs for the elite performers. I particularly wanted to reward the highest producers. In sales, for example, that meant people who attained 200 percent of goal, not merely 100 percent. So we formed the President's Council, a club that not only financially rewarded high achievement, but which was wired into the decision making in the company. Thus through this recognition came *influence,* which is another way to compensate people.

We created clubs to acknowledge rainmakers in every department. Administration/personnel had the Winner's Circle; sales support had the Tiger's Club; the technical development teams received the MSA Cup. Prominence is an excellent way to motivate people: those who don't get it, aspire to; and those who do, don't want to lose it. Ego.

Perks

When it's financially realistic, perks are an important way to compensate rainmakers. Perks materially support prominence. They add dimension to the loftiest corporate and personal goals, and substance to just making a list of achievers. In short, they make people *die* to get them and keep them. MSA sent the President's Council members to Hawaii for four days. Basically, for those four days, we spoiled them like sheiks, making sure they knew that at the end they were expected to return to the jungle, claws extended. They rented Maseratis, flew helicopters over volcanos, were rubbed down in spas, played golf on the cliffs of Maui, and sipped a little Dom Perignon. Membership in the President's Council became the ultimate reward for the ultimate achievement.

We insisted that their spouses (or significant others) accompany them. There are compelling reasons to do it this way. One is because it's vital to have recognition at that level. We wanted the families to understand that we regarded the sellers' achievements as the high-water mark of excellence, and that we regarded their support as being integral to those achievements.

We wanted them to know that they were part of the MSA family. When we said, "People are the key," it meant them too. We presented each wife with a diamond on a gold necklace (women sellers also got the diamonds and necklaces). Each year they or their spouses made the President's Council, they would receive two more diamonds. The event not only forged relationships with the spouses, but it turned them into active goal sharers.

The truth is, MSA's jungle rules asked a lot of its sellers. Anytime you've based your career on relationships instead of transactions, you can no longer clock out at 5 P.M. You do whatever it takes, including midnight calls, long hours on the road, and passing through a haze of time zones. A lot of sacrifice is asked of families. You just have to recognize it.

Of course, perks don't have to be as opulent as the President's Council affairs. Give someone a parking place with his or her name on it. Give them a higher-payoff insurance policy. Give them and their partners tickets on a dinner train. We once had a caricaturist draw everyone who had made a club, then put them all onto a poster. It became enormously popular. When we handed them out, everyone went from table to table like school children to get them signed, then hung them in their offices. Obviously, perks need to be tailored to the resources of a given company. But if you use some imagination, you can still do inexpensively what perks are supposed to do: tell someone you *recognize* what they did and want to *reward* it.

Promotions

Whenever you take the time to identify the rainmakers, you need to ask: Are they where they should be in the company? The fact that MSA's management engaged the President's Council throughout the year on policy, operations, and other tough discussions, gave us a wonderful opportunity to find the next generation of managers. Fully 50 percent of the President's Council members went on to management positions. If you're creating a compensation *environment,* promotions are vital because they often encompass the goals you've committed to share with someone. It always has to be the right person in the right job, of course, but when you're picking from a family of tigers, the success rate is astronomical.

DON'T MAUL ANOTHER TIGER

Confession time. Ever since my apocalyptic breakfast with Jay Forrester, I've gone to great lengths—some would say extremes, and might be right—to recognize and compensate people. I've always believed that my success is whatever *they've* done, so it's never been hard for me to share the wealth once MSA had some.

But one of the difficulties of bestowing so much recognition on the elite is that the not-yet-elite sometimes feel left out or offended or both. During my own learning process, I made some brutal mistakes, which I herewith share.

Early in my MSA days, I decided to recognize tigers using a technique that had actually become something of a tradition when I'd been at Honeywell. At the annual dinner, every seller was given a badge that was one of two colors. They didn't know what the badges were colored for, but in fact one color designated those who had made goal; the other, those who had not.

We tried this at MSA. When the waitresses came around with dinner, they gave steak to the wearers of one color and beans to wearers of the other. From the looks of horror, you would have thought we'd served up roadkill. A lot of people were indignantly saying, "We've worked hard! We're all winners!"

The lesson was simple: Don't embarrass, even lightheartedly, people who have gathered for honors. It's not that they expect so much to be honored—sellers in particular know exactly where they stand—but they just don't want to be singled out in public for not being honored, especially in the presence of those who are getting awards.

We never tried that again, although I still believe in the value of publicly posting performance figures. On the one hand, this does put pressure on sellers not to allow themselves to be seen at the bottom. But more important, it gives others in the company the chance to help those who find themselves there. And there are a lot fewer complaints than with bean dinners.

Another mistake I made was in trying to recognize the mega-achievers in the President's Council and failing to recognize lesser—though still significant—selling. By allowing membership only for sellers who made 200 percent of goal, I neglected those who had made 100 percent. Some even felt like failures, and after doing exactly what they were supposed to do. That was just wrong. So we created a 100 Percent Club to make certain they knew that we knew they'd been significant contributors. They got four-day trips to Phoenix or Las Vegas instead of Hawaii, but the gesture made a world of difference.

Never let goal performances go unrecognized.

Of course, there are some people you're not going to make happy even with the best intentions and results. The only thing you can do when you encounter the chronic grump is nice 'em to death, then move on by.

Without a doubt, the most tirelessly mauling beast I ever encountered was Grant Fitts, a man who energetically lived up to his last name. Imagine a very old tiger that had not purred in years, but instead roared even the most insignificant of requests, such as, "Coffee!" Fitts was the chairman of Gulf Life Insurance, one of the secured creditors of MSA when I took it over. He was a walking object lesson in insensitivity training. He was in his sixties at the time and very much wanted back the $3 million he'd invested in MSA.

I got a sense of his style when he called me from his headquarters in Jacksonville, Florida, and demanded that I drop everything and fly down there instantly to meet him. I did. When I got there, I was put in a waiting room. He called in one of his managers and asked where some Texas-based sales manager was. "He's on vacation, fishing," the fellow told him.

"Well, there's a plane in Dallas," screamed Fitts. "I want him found and on it in an hour!"

Then he told one of his managers to take me to lunch and he'd talk to me later. We met when I got back. It was instructive. I had no *idea* there were so many ways I could be sued. During the meeting, a secretary came in and told him that the vacationing manager had been found and was in the waiting room. "I just wanted to get his attention!" growled Fitts. "Put him on the next plane back to Texas! *Tourist!*"

My ears were ringing for a month. A couple of years later, I was excited to finally be doing something that would bring a smile to Fitts's face. I had a check for the $2.1 million balance for him, payment in full. It was an amount he would have gotten a fraction of if I'd just liquidated MSA. As I gave it to him, expecting whatever constituted a rush of gratitude, he looked at me with icy eyes. "Why didn't you *wire* this money?" he roared. *"Do you know how much interest we lost in the two hours it took you to deliver this?"*

I just smiled, thanked him for not stoning me, and left. I was thinking: *If I ever need a heart transplant, I'll get Grant's—it's never been used.* From that day to this, I've never raised my voice to an employee.

LET NO ONE GO UNNOTICED

In the bush, tigers live by these kinds of hypersenses that make it almost impossible for another creature to slip past them unnoticed. That's the level of sensitivity tigers in business need to cultivate in their relationships. It leads to a jungle truth that is subtle, almost paradoxical: *Not everyone can be recognized, but no one must go unnoticed.*

One potential problem in a high-achievement–high-reward environment is that not everyone makes the honor roll. When everyone is graded on a curve, there is always the risk that those on the wrong side of the bell will get demoralized. You always hope that they will use that situation to set higher goals and achieve greater things, but sometimes it doesn't automatically work that way. And you can't artificially create pseudo-honors just so people can say they "made it," or you instantly devalue your whole compensation system.

That leaves you invariably with people who have not been formally recognized. That in itself is fine, and in fact necessary. Then the question is: Having lavished so much on the rainmakers, what do I do for everyone else?

And the answer is: You treat them with all the warmth you would have for the most conspicuous achiever in the company. No exceptions. The most important thing is to regard every person as an individual, regardless of his or her position in the company or the honors they might have received.

In a commencement speech recently at Mercer University, I put it this way: "The secret of relating to people is simple: As you greet them, treat that person as if he or she, for that one moment, is the only person in the world. If people realize you care and are interested in them, they in turn will respond positively to you, and, through them, you will grow."

When I meet people, I'm often asked what I do. I always say, "I'm a worker, like everyone else." It's no different from the way it is with my heroes on the gridiron, the Atlanta Falcons. You've got tight ends, down linemen, wide receivers, and quarterbacks. Everybody has a job to do. In business, I'm just the coach, no better or worse than anyone else.

So take a little time to be a coach. Talk to everyone. Remind them that they wouldn't be working for you unless they had what it took, because you only hire extraordinary people. Ask them if they have everything they need. Ask them if they are being adequately supported. Ask them what *you* can do for *them*. And tell them you look forward to seeing them next year in Hawaii (or wherever you honor rainmakers).

The challenge for managers isn't to have a company in which everyone is at 200 percent of goal. That's just not realistic. But you can get close to a goal that is almost as difficult: getting everyone to realize considerably more of their potential.

If you've done the hiring right for your corporate den, you've got people who are creative, passionate, honest, resourceful, and aggressive. They have the raw materials to do a lot for themselves and for the company. Sometimes the missing piece is a small one—a lateral move to a different job to which they're better suited; a practical demonstration of the distant boundaries in which tigers can operate; a firsthand look at the real-life use of autonomy; or just the right words of confidence from a manager or coworker.

If your hiring process is right, then everyone can contribute. That—and the fact that they all are human beings whose lives are entwined with yours—is why no one should go unnoticed.

BEWARE THE ROGUE TIGERS

It might be because I'm naive, but I've gotten through life liking almost everyone I've met. Maybe it's because I look for the good in people and have gotten pretty fair at finding it. If I know I'm going to dislike someone, I generally write him out of my life. Dislike requires just too much negative energy. And using that kind of energy—contempt, regret, rage, worry—is a complete waste of time.

Over the years, in the cause of developing initiative in people, I've done a lot of forgiving (and often asked for forgiveness). But the closest I come to disliking a group of people is when they are dishonest or exploitative. I don't keep those people around me long.

There is so much asked and given in a Jungle Rules environment—initiatives, tactics, imagination—that a code of conduct is imperative, but it isn't always easy to enforce. The characteristics of business tigers—particularly aggressiveness, energy, and autonomy—can bring people into the den who just can't quite make out the uncrossable lines. These are the rogue tigers.

In MSA's early years, we turned loose that energy and, while we made a lot of sales, some sellers also developed a kind of Wild Bunch reputation. The loosest cannons among them were called gunslingers—sellers who could burn through a territory brilliantly during the day, then release unspent energy swinging on hotel chandeliers at night.

We wanted to control the gunslingers' fire without extinguishing it, so we laid down our code of conduct, which at least kept people off the chandeliers, if not from expending that wonderful energy in other ways. Along the way we forgave a lot. We never penalized event-related failure, though chronic performance problems were dealt with directly (no one is ever happy failing day after day). Apart from that, dishonesty and exploitation were the reddest of flags.

Dishonesty requires only the universal rule you surely already have. If someone is dishonest, you put as much Mother Earth between them and you as possible.

The harder ones to call sometimes are the exploiters, the manipulators of the gray area, the people whose abuses can erode morale little by little. It's a situation made worse by the fact that they often feel invulnerable because their contribution to the company is both big and conspicuous.

It is one of the small pitfalls of a high-reward environment. If you don't take some action immediately, it will destroy the "compensation lifestyle" you've created. And the abusers can come from anywhere—including the President's Council, whose members would seem to have it all.

Remember, this is a group of sellers who attained 200 percent of goal and earned trips to Hawaii with their spouses or significant others. They get the most royal of treatment, as the most well-heeled of sellers, but every once in a while, for the isolated individual—perhaps 1 or 2 percent of the players—that isn't enough.

We had a fellow who decided one evening to take a bath. The problem was the bath was in Dom Perignon, at about $150 a bottle. He charged it to his room, which meant the company paid for this little cleansing. Another gentleman took the Maserati we'd rented for him and proceeded to roll it over in a state whose speed limits make that hard to do.

We had one super salesman who simply loved the ladies. He had had an office romance in Atlanta that led to my reassigning him to California. Thirty days after he moved there, I flew out to work on a deal with him. He walked up to me at the airport from his open-topped Mercedes, with a sweater tied around his neck, his hair permed back, and sunglasses on. I sort of had a sense it was all over.

It turned out that he was indeed romancing a young female marketing assistant on his expense account. To make his indiscretion worse, she had been living with a lawyer who made some trouble by sending the company a letter threatening a sexual harassment action. And, by the way, our super salesman was married. There was no place for him in MSA, whatever his sales achievements.

A high-reward environment demands an honor system. People generally don't begrudge money and perks to genuine achievers because none of us would be here without them. But the integrity of the compensation system is in serious trouble when the prominent and successful people begin to abuse it.

Part of the compensation for everyone is that you don't allow abusers to succeed.

SHARE THE KILL

When tigers in the bush have, so to speak, brought home dinner for the evening, more often than not they share the feast, at least with other tigers. Substitute the word "wealth" for "kill," and you have a comparable premise for tigers in business.

I'm not talking about a paycheck, I'm talking about the *wealth*. Whether your company is public or private, you should think about how to make owners of as many key people as possible.

Business tigers in particular are stirred to their souls by the prospect of ownership. Competitive instincts become fiercer, imagination becomes more acute, persistence becomes a little more tireless. The small details that might remain undealt with by a nonowner are carefully handled. Ownership, even in small increments, generates emotional and intellectual adrenalin.

I remember how motivated I was to own a business. It was easy for me to think others could be similarly moved by the idea of stock or partnership. Particularly in the early years, when there was little money to spend and little latitude to operate, we had to make sure that everything was done with care, with precision, and without waste. So we gave ten key employees stock in the company—1 percent ownership for each.

To this day, I think it was one of the best management moves we've ever made. But the initial reaction was pure skepticism. The employees had had stock in MSA before the bankruptcy—stock then worth less than the paper it was printed on. Still I was surprised at the reception my offer got.

After I had passed out the stock certificates with great pride and waited for the flood of gratitude and inspiration to wash over me, a new form of competition broke out: paper airplanes. People were folding the certificates into intricate aerodynamic creations and sailing them around the room.

In truth, it took a couple of years before people began going home, unfolding their airplanes, and putting them in a safe deposit box. After we had several profitable periods—for a number of years, we nearly doubled revenue annually—I gave a presentation in which I tried to envision the next phase of MSA. I showed the group a slide of the beautiful new Simmons Mattress building in Atlanta, superimposing MSA's name at the top of the building. "Someday we'll have our own building," I told them. Their views of ownership had come around.

Those "airplanes" were eventually worth about $3.3 million each. Even with the skepticism we waded through in the early days, everybody came through on the details we needed to survive. Everyone behaved like an owner, even if it took awhile to realize they might really *become* one.

When the stock certificates began to appreciate dramatically in the mid '70s, the ownership mentality really took root. People realized they were working not only for a paycheck, but for something greater—a business, an estate, a share of the wealth. The depth of their interest in every issue, every policy, every new product, every new seller, the tiniest turn of the smallest cog in the machine, was manifold over what it might have been as an "employee."

In the bush, tigers like to believe they own some territory. In the business jungle, tigers feel the same way. And they'll fight for it with a ferocity you could never get from someone just passing through.

JUNGLE RULE SUMMARY

IF YOU CAPTURE DINNER, YOU GET TO EAT IT.

Them that does, gets. Reward the rainmakers.

MAKE COMPENSATION A LIFESTYLE, NOT A PAYCHECK

Money pays bills; a "compensation lifestyle" helps people achieve goals.

JUNGLE RULES

DON'T MAUL ANOTHER TIGER

If you're not careful, motivation can backfire.

LET NO ONE GO UNNOTICED

Treat every person you meet as if he or she is the only person in the world.

BEWARE THE ROGUE TIGERS

Don't hesitate to deal with the bad seeds.

SHARE THE KILL

As tigers like territory, so business tigers like ownership.

10

Jungle Rule #10:
If a competitor is stalking you, extinction
will not.

Competition. The heart of free enterprise The soul of innovation. The adrenalin in the hunt for business. But competition is other things as well. It is the most schizophrenic aspect of business. The source of more disinformation than the old Kremlin. And the root cause of tremendous expense. So what are we to make of competition?

Cherish it.

Competition is sustenance. Competition breeds better people, better products, better processes and ideas. Competition drives thinking to a level that passive monopoly could never hope to achieve. Competition is the antidote to lethargy. It focuses the mind, ignites the imagination, rallies the team, and unites everyone. How could anyone not like competition?

We always took the approach at MSA that the goal of business shouldn't be a world without competition, but competitors without a prayer. It should be to build such a program that its very success is intimidating. Competition is what people need in their lives to survive in the jungle.

Knowing this, what should you do with competitors once they've begun stalking you? Answer: You pick out the fiercest and give it a face.

Most businesses are surrounded by a crowded field of competitors, some bigger, some smaller, each with distinguishing marks. But in the majority of companies, few or none rise to become the *personification* of competition. The enemy in name and deed. The prey. The sustenance.

Competition needs a name and a face.

MSA was in the same business for over two decades, selling financial and accounting software (although we expanded into many other areas as well). Over the years, our competitive focus changed many times as we put new faces on the enemy, as we found someone new to psych up for—someone new to hate, to stalk, to defeat. Doug MacIntyre, one of our top sales managers, put it like this: "My view was that the people I competed with had a mission in life: It was to keep my kids from going to college and having a good meal." And the schizophrenic aspect of all this?

Out of the jungle, I love most of my competitors like family. I play golf with them, dine with them, work with them on industry issues, and extend every courtesy of the respectful relationship. But back in the jungle, we go after one another like ancient enemies.

If you want to be the best you can be, you *need* someone who is trying to prevent you from doing that. That's not always easy to do, but it is essential to do. I offer the following story about competing—hunting for the enemy—in the software business, though the rules would apply in any other industry.

In MSA's early days, when there were relatively few competing software companies in existence, we could almost have declared an oligopoly. The idea of software "products" was new. In many instances, we weren't competing with another software company for the sale. More often, it was fear of the unknown. But we couldn't personify "the unknown." We needed a focus, an enemy, a predator with a face who was out to do us in.

We found him back then in the data processing manager, who was doing his dead-level best to cultivate that fear of the unknown. This was the person who oversaw all of that software development—invariably at great cost—inside the empire he'd built at the company.

Data processing managers almost universally resented software companies in those days. They reasoned (myopically) that if companies could buy software, then the DP manager's job was in jeopardy. They invented the Not-Invented-Here Syndrome, which said if the software wasn't developed on site, there might be no one around to fix its problems, maintain it, and enhance it—especially if the software company went out of business.

By picking up on their arguments, we are able to personify the enemy. We could attach faces and even names. We could direct our marketing to other (higher) decision makers and focus our attack on "business problems" instead of "computer problems." But while we often circumvented the data processing managers in our selling, we knew we'd need them eventually. So we also did things to educate them about products, to get them into the fold and make them see that software products could make them a hero, not steal their jobs.

As the data processing managers grew to see software products as tools during the '70s, the number of software companies started to skyrocket. No arena became more populated with competitors than accounting and financial software for IBM computers. There literally were hundreds of serious players.

When that new scenario evolved, we changed the face of the enemy. For a while, we changed it so much, we talked about the Competitor of the Month. The idea was not to focus on the whole marketplace, but on the biggest (or loudest or toughest) *player* in the marketplace at any given time.

Things changed quickly in the software world. A new player would start talking about some new tweak that represented "a revolution" and drew attention to itself. They then became the enemies, the predators, and drew all of our attention. When someone else knocked them off, we changed the face again. The enemy *al-*

ways had a name and a face, and wasn't just a formless blob called "the competition."

But fighting the Competitor of the Month was never as intense as facing down a tenured enemy, someone we could despise with relish. Our most enduring competitor over two decades was McCormack & Dodge Corporation, located in Natick, Massachusetts. M & D was the perfect enemy. It was a good firm, with sound technology and competent management; it understood the software business and had aggressive sellers. Gradually we began to see that more and more sales were coming down to MSA and M & D.

But best of all M & D also had the wisdom to personify its competition, and for them, that personification was MSA. This was perfect for us. In talking to prospects, they almost always put their products up against ours, to the exclusion of the rest of the companies. This left the impression with prospects that MSA must be a pretty fair enterprise to get all this attention.

Victories over MSA were celebrated euphorically, as were ours over M & D. It was the Packers versus the Bears, the Yankees versus the Red Sox. They hated us and we hated them. It was wonderful.

Some years later, in one of the great ironies in this business, McCormack & Dodge was merged with MSA to form Dun & Bradstreet Software. When the deal was done, I held a teleconference with our sellers in the field to announce it to them. There was a long pause, as if signifying disbelief. Then the lone voice of Brent Wells, a salesman in our southern region, spoke for everyone:

"Who do we hate now?"

Every Ali needs a Frazier, every Schwarzkopf needs a Saddam, and every company needs a McCormack & Dodge. When you find the best competitor out there, make them your only one.

NICE 'EM TO DEATH

Fangs and claws are not the only weapons by which tigers survive, in business or in the bush. Sometimes the most disarming weapon is civility.

When I was younger, I was pretty quick to go into head-to-head confrontation. If someone yelled, I yelled back. If someone got mad, then I got mad. You make the rules, I'll play the game. But of course that always left me playing by their rules. It was about then that I learned that tigers, which are known for their terrifying roar, do it very rarely.

Once during hearings in a lawsuit, I found myself face-to-face with an attorney who called me "a liar." I am many things, but liar is not one of them. I stood and started an angry shouting match with the attorney, who had probably gotten the reaction he'd wanted from me. The judge threatened to hold both of us in contempt. My lawyer thought that retreat was the better part of valor, so we left and returned to his law office. It was the beginning of one of the great moments of my life.

He took me into one of the back offices. There, sitting in a wheelchair, was this small, thin, hunched figure. I knew him instantly. It was Robert Tyre Jones, Jr., "Bob" to virtually everyone, the finest golfer ever to split a fairway. The man who had been my hero since I took up golf as a child. Once the picture of vigor and athleticism when he dominated his sport in the '20s, Jones now seemed to be shrinking under the weight of a debilitating spinal disease. But there was still a lively spark in his eyes, and this wonderful, calm wisdom in his voice.

He was then a partner in the law firm, and he had become almost as revered for his legal skills as he had been for his golf. Knowing that Jones was my idol, my lawyer introduced me to him and explained what had happened that day in court.

"You know," Jones said, "I used to lose my temper with every bad shot. Once during the British Open in Scotland, I was playing the Old Course at St. Andrews. The course had gotten the best of me. Finally I took an eleven on Number Twelve. I tore my scorecard in half, threw down my clubs, and walked away.

"After that, I began to think my temper was my trouble. When I finally got it under control, I began to win. My advice is, don't ever let someone do that to you again."

Jones's invaluable advice became a lifestyle for me, both in business and outside of it. I've long said of business, "It's only a game." You play hard and you play to win, but, as in life, the wrong emotions are simply destructive. As ferociously as we pursue business, there is no competitor I can really say I've spent even a moment with in personal confrontation or anger. In fact, I value my relationships with all of them. If someone looks like he has something on his mind, I try to ease it out of him with gentle discussion.

If a competitor has done something that starts to genuinely make you mad—a blatant lie ignites most people—you still should try not to get angry. Instead, convert the energy. Turn it into greater persistence, greater imagination, greater resourcefulness. You calmly correct the misinformation, especially to the prospect. The next time you see the competitor, it's easy to smile, to shake hands, to nice 'em to death, because you probably walked away with the order. And your humanity.

Bob Jones, who died some months after we met, was right. At the end of the day, the battle done, it is civility that makes someone a winner.

LIE PERFECTLY STILL AND LISTEN TO THE ENEMY

No one criticizes you quite like a competitor. If you have a wart, they'll make you a witch. They will find a thousand niggling grains of sand to dump into the prospect's soup. What you need to do is listen for the sand in *their* soup. What comes up more than anything else? What single thing annoys them most? What do they go to the greatest trouble to denigrate? When you know that, you've got a valuable insight. Because that's usually what prospects like about you and keep bringing up.

MSA's mission from the outset was simply stated: "To be a successful and profitable software services company with a personal touch." It was a theme that was important to us, and certainly to me personally. We'd always believed that people were more important than technology, even in the technology industry. But there was always the chance that customers wouldn't see things that way.

From the beginning MSA adopted its "People Are the Key" theme. We oriented marketing and advertising to people themes, and always stressed people, people, people to prospects. People as software developers. People as management leaders. People as support providers. People as sharers of goals.

Our staunchest competitor, McCormack & Dodge, was utterly fixated on technology. M & D had hired some truly superb technologists, always stressed the "leading edge" in its marketing, thought in terms of software revolutions, and only rarely had a real person in its advertising. Its sellers talked bits and bytes and features and functions and "state of the art." They exerted a great deal of energy deriding MSA's software as "average," and loved to tell people we weren't "a software company, but a marketing company."

In truth, I would stand our software technically up against theirs anytime. But I was more interested in the efforts they made to put down our theme of "people." We would call on a client and say, in effect, that you're not buying software, you're buying 3,000 people, twenty-four hours a day, who are going to share your goals.

Then M & D would come in and start pitching sheer technology. We interpreted their message as being not that the client would win the race, but that he'd have the fastest bike on the block. There's a difference. Understanding that difference gave us the edge.

When we saw how the "people" theme drove M & D up the wall, we knew we'd tapped into a vein. We knew customers were opting for the people approach—simplicity in the software, ease of use, versatility, support, goal sharing—over the exotic technology approach. M & D had probably been successful in establishing itself as a more advanced technology company, and yet prospects were often dealing them out in favor of "that marketing company."

M & D was pulling its hair out. It created "Keybuster" awards for sellers who won out over MSA in a sale. At company meetings, employees actually did *skits* deriding MSA's technology. They even made papier-mâché masks of me (one was sent to me). I loved it.

The more conspicuously frustrated M & D became, the more dedicated we became to our theme. We knew if the number one competitor was hearing this, so were all the others. Sometimes the best consultant you can find is the one you'd least expect.

LET THE STRAY CATS COME HOME

George Steinbrenner was right about Billy Martin. You *can* go home again.

One of the good things about not holding a grudge (even against a competitor) is that you can get acquainted with people—sometimes excellent people—whom the vengeful would have rejected forever. It's the old adage about cutting off your nose and all that. But the operating premise of building a corporate tigers' den is that you first surround yourself with extraordinary people. That means keeping your options open about where you find them.

Early on when we were reorganizing MSA, a number of good employees left in anger. Many of them began formulating plans to start their own company to take on MSA. They said lots of indelicate things about Gene Kelly and me, and competitively—maybe literally—would have loved to bury us.

One of the most strident defectors was Dennis Vohs, an extremely bright young manager who thought I'd personally derailed his career. I don't think anyone wanted to see me crash as much as did Vohs. But I understood his perspective and held no grudges. (Okay, I confess to the tiniest pang of ironic joy when Vohs, during one of the combat meetings, was bitten by a pet monkey and had to get a couple of stitches.)

After about four months, the start-up effort dissolved. Vohs called me and asked to come back. I was faced with an interesting business dilemma: Do I hire back someone who, while talented, has already demonstrated that he is not above taking a walk and planning my demise? Or do I turn him out after making a cruel joke about man-eating monkeys?

Answer: Business is business, and Vohs had the makings of a tiger. I took him back.

I'd never taken much of what the Vohs coterie said personally. One of the foundation stones of good relationships is empathy, and I knew why some of the old guard felt as they did. I *had* caused trauma. I *had* disrupted things. I *had* been the agent of radical change. Good or bad, life wasn't going to be the same.

The challenge for me was to figure out if someone who had been so stridently opposed to me could rechannel that emotion into productive energy. Could he be as dedicated as tigers need to be? Could he resist the lure of other competitors for long? Was he looking for a paycheck or a commitment?

When I asked around about Vohs, people said his talent surpassed his emotion (and he had a lot of emotion). I didn't want to let a grudge muck things up, and I didn't believe he was spying. So I concluded that even if his commitment was tentative at first, I could strengthen it over time; I could make a believer of him.

Dennis Vohs ended up staying with MSA for seventeen years and led many parts of the company.

There is always some risk in bringing in an outsider with ties to a competitor. But when the stray cats come home, especially the gifted ones, don't turn them out automatically. Often their bad business decisions were nothing more than that, and we all make them. It comes back to two management tools for tigers: *autonomy* and *forgiveness*. If someone makes an independent decision that doesn't pan out, you always say—to the right person—okay, let's try again.

IMAGINATION MAKES THE KILLER INSTINCT FUN

The only reason to compete is to win. You don't get into business for aerobics or transcendental enlightenment. You do it to usefully create, sell, and profit better than the competition, all while solving someone's problems.

And to have a good time doing it.

Few things gave MSA's tigers greater joy than using their imagination to drive competitors up the tree. It was one thing to buy a lot of advertising and dominate a publication, something anyone can do if they have the money; it was something else entirely to go head to head in a more or less equal forum, such as a trade show or a convention. It was there that imagination got its greatest workout and provided its happiest rewards.

Our objective was simple: Get all of the attention of all of the convention-goers all of the time.

Ambitious? Well, that's how we thought, anyway. In effect, we wanted simultaneously to capture the audience for MSA and remove it entirely from the grasp of the enemy. This would accomplish our two objectives of getting the sales from attendees and destroying the morale of competitors. It was psychological warfare as much as business.

At one American Bankers Association Automation Conference we attended in Houston, our booth was smaller than most, and the others were more expensive. The challenge was to find a way to get attendees to overlook everyone else and spend their time with us.

Our major competitor at the time was University Computing Company, a hugely successful software firm out of Dallas. With the conference in Houston, UCC figured it had a virtual home-court advantage. MSA, on the other hand, had only two clients in Houston, the Houston National Bank and the First City National Bank.

Just getting people into our booth wasn't enough. We needed to keep them away from UCC's flashier booth and legions of staffers. Dennis Vohs got a group of MSA people together and came up with the idea of using our two Houston-based customers as live demonstration sites. To make the tour exciting, we hired a helicopter to land on the roof of the convention center and ferry people to the first site, where they could watch MSA's software in action. Then a limousine would take them to the second site for another tour. Drinks and food were provided during the tour.

The whole trip took the better part of the day. But we had made it so much fun that almost every attendee signed up for it. When they weren't away on the tour, they were standing in line near MSA's booth waiting for the helicopter to pick them up. UCC's people were pulling out their hair—an expensive booth, packed with staffers, and no one to show their products to.

Practically every attendee was in our captive audience for hours, getting back just as the show was closing, too late to want to hear anything from anyone else. Every time the helicopter took off—we had it land and depart within earshot of the booths—you could see the UCC folks bristle. It was a joyous scene.

Over the years, we used similar tactics hundreds of times to gain the attention of our audience. Some of the best attractions were magicians, orangutans, celebrities such as Fran Tarkenton and Tommy Lasorda, and models on waterbeds, which is a story in itself (see "Motivating the Tigers," chapter 4). It just takes some imagination, some daring, and a strategic desire to "own" an audience. Never think small.

Once you get your audience, of course, you have to have a story for them; you have to show them how you can make their lives better. If you can't do that, then all of that fun of capturing your audience is just a prelude to failure. And you're in this to win.

JUNGLE RULE SUMMARY

IF A COMPETITOR IS STALKING YOU, EXTINCTION WILL NOT.

If you have no competition, invent some, because they'll push you to be your best.

JUNGLE RULES

NICE 'EM TO DEATH

There is no contradiction between playing ferociously to win and keeping your civility, even to those you dislike.

LIE PERFECTLY STILL AND LISTEN TO THE ENEMY

The greatest insights to your strengths come from the unlikeliest of sources.

LET THE STRAY CATS COME HOME

Don't discount opening your den to a former enemy.

IMAGINATION MAKES THE KILLER INSTINCT FUN

There is no greater joy than using your wits to send the enemy up a tree.

11

RELATIONSHIPS FOR FUN AND PROFIT

Jungle Rule #11:
Build a front porch on your treehouse.

The business of relationships—and the relationships of business—are the two recurring themes of the jungle, as well as of this book. It was well-cultivated relationships that took MSA from near-oblivion to the top of the software world within ten years. What follows here is some of what we learned.

For the last four centuries, until thirty years ago, people built homes with front porches. The idea was to have a place to engage the world firsthand—to watch the activity, to speak with neighbors, to develop relationships in the world we all shared together.

Then something happened. People began turning away. Homes were built not with porches in the front but with decks in the back. Privacy fences went up. Now many of us live in "neighborhoods" in which we don't know the neighbors, and "porches" have become small squares on which you wipe your feet.

The same thing has happened to business.

Some people contend that you should never build a front porch on your business. There is a school of thought that says personal relationships in business are to be avoided at all costs. Don't hire or do business with friends or relatives. The operative phrase is "clinical detachment." If you maintain the corporate class society—management as royalty, employees and customers as faceless masses, policy by dictum—then it's easier to do the dirty work, to separate yourself from someone else's troublesome aspirations, and to sleep like a baby on your deck out back.

All true—at least until the neighbors revolt.

In February 1984, *Business Week* ran an in-depth story on what was then America's most admired company, IBM Corporation. IBM and the magazine speculated (on the cover, no less) that, by 1994, Big Blue would be a $185 billion corporation. They missed by more than $120 billion. One primary reason was IBM's atrophied relationships.

IBM's steep plunge came chiefly because the company had gotten so big and bureaucratic that it could no longer relate to its customers' needs. It was driven more by its self-history—whatever IBM manufactures will be bought by 70 percent of the computing world—than by customers' needs to reduce the size of their computers and the size of their computer expenditures. It had become a sumo wrestler in pinstripes, doing battle with a flock of hummingbirds. It had separated itself from its clients' troublesome aspirations. And while it lurched and staggered, Microsoft and Apple (among others) shifted, darted, and attacked.

The key is simple: *Keep your big company small.* Bigness and bureaucracy work to separate human beings and both happen in almost every company. People distance themselves from their neighbors, employee from manager, manager from executive, executive from customer. Everything is by the numbers, eye contact is taboo, personal inquiries are meticulously avoided. The result is a cold, gray, impersonal experience for which few people can muster affection, loyalty, or exuberant effort, which most businesses need to succeed.

Contributing to this is a lot of misused technology. Businesses have at their disposal wondrous tools of communication and analysis. The tools themselves are neither good nor evil, but merely instruments. Properly used, tools such as voice mail, fax machines, personal computers, electronic memos, and the myriad products for computerized analyses can measurably enhance relationships. Misused, however, they can contribute mightily to the dereliction of personal relationships that business needs to return to.

While you need a front porch for your business—the mentality, facilities, and procedures to interact one-on-one with employees and customers—you also need to get out. Professor Marty Marshal of Harvard Business School used to say, "Take a walk down Third Avenue." Third Avenue was his metaphor for the street, for real life, for getting out, getting dirty, and seeing firsthand how people think and act. A walk down Third Avenue not only provides insights not commonly available in, say, bar charts, but like a front porch, it gives you a place to build relationships—including some that might not make it to your porch.

At MSA, we stressed incessant *personal interaction*. As one of America's largest software companies, we had every electronic tool in the world at our disposal. We could have buried ourselves so deeply in the technology cocoon that no one could have found us without a password. But we always emphasized human contact.

The top priority was in-person conversation. Second priority was direct telephone contact. The key word in relationships is *interaction*, and most gadgetry doesn't allow that. The idea was to live in the skin of whomever we wanted a relationship with; to get into such synchronization with their thinking, their plans, and their goals that we would never make a misstep that would hurt them.

Tools declined in value the further they removed us from the individual. That went for manager-employee relationships, strategist-marketplace relationships, service-customer relationships, MSA-supplier relationships—any scenario in which human beings needed an interchange. Throughout my business career, the only concession I ever made to technology in my office has been a telephone. The rest of the office is like a front porch. Lots of chairs, a big table, and a couple of sofas, all designed for conversation, for interaction, for going person to person. During its history, MSA has had about

16,000 employees. At one time or another, I've had them all to my front porch, or I've visited theirs.

A front porch, with its panoramic view of what's going on, is a great place to remember that people are the key. And as long as you have one, even the biggest business can stay small enough to succeed.

RELATIONSHIPS ARE IN THE DETAILS

One of the most inspiring people I ever met is a man named Charlie Yates. A legend in Georgia, he was one of America's great amateur golfers back in the 1930s and '40s. When he retired from his business career in 1984, he was called "one of the four pillars of Atlanta—Margaret Mitchell, Bobby Jones, Coca-Cola, and Charlie Yates." Margaret, Bobby, and Coke never were in better company.

But it wasn't his career or prominence that mattered. Charlie has an utter genius for civility and genuineness that would have seen him succeed in any profession. He speaks in his gentle, front-porch, Atlanta drawl and loves to relate stories about the thing he holds dearest to his heart—friendships. His business career—"I'm a salesman. I was a salesman even when I played golf. It's the best profession to make friends"—is a massive collection of nurtured friendships spanning eight decades. What he demonstrated was how to take business relationships beyond acquaintance and into affection. You read it right—affection.

Charlie's propensity for striking up friendships comes completely naturally to him. It wasn't something he did just for business, though the payoffs came back to him time and again. He tells a story of the time, back in the lean years, when he was competing in the Western Open Golf Tournament in Peoria, Illinois.

"I was playing with a friend of mine from Oklahoma named Walter Emery and a pro by the name of Jud McSpaden. There were three of us standing on the first tee. This gentleman, whom I perceived to be rather elderly, was standing by himself swinging a club.

I asked him if he would like to join us. He said he would. He told us his name was Burton Peek from Moline, Illinois.

"Afterward, Mr. Peek said, 'I want to take you boys to town.' Well, we were staying down at the YMCA for two seventy-five a week, so we thought that was fine. He bought us a nice steak, which was something we hadn't seen in quite a long time.

"Two years later, I was working in the credit department for First National Bank in Atlanta, analyzing financial statements. I had one from Deere & Company, a big farm implement company. It said, 'Chairman, Burton F. Peek.' So I wrote and asked him if he was the same Burton Peek who had played golf with us two years ago. He said he was, then came out to see me. He hadn't forgotten.

"At that time all the business that Deere was doing in Atlanta was with another bank. Pretty soon, he gave us part of that business. Later I saw Mr. Peek in England, and he said, 'I've transferred all of our business to you.' All of that friendship really started because we saw this lonely man there at the tee and thought it would be nice if he joined us. You just never know when your opportunities are going to come along."

MAKE IT PERSONAL

People in business often make the mistake of trying to fabricate relationships instead of trying to grow them. Few gestures are more hollow than the "personalized" letter written by the automatic handwriting device. This is the cursive way of saying "occupant." Yet millions are sent all over the world.

Can any of these artificial creations even register on the appreciation scale? Not for anyone I've ever asked. Every one of your communications should make the needle jump. Everything else is a waste of time and money, unless your objective was to paper the birdcage.

If someone personally contacts you, they are due a personal response. Try the simple personal call, something our faxes and electronic memos are removing us from. I've always been amazed by the vast number of people who never take the time to do it. I've seen executives who have been smitten by their own self-importance and decide that their secretaries can make and return their calls. People read their mail, check their phone messages, peruse their memos, then delegate responses to everyone but themselves. If the press calls, public relations gets the nod. Wall Street? Give it to finance. Customer? The service department is there to serve. Employee? What do we pay human resources to do? We've bureaucratized ourselves into the artful dodgers of human relationships.

The telephone, one of our oldest office tools, still is one of the most important because it's *personal*. The key is discipline. Make your conversations friendly but *brief*. No one will be offended; even a brief conversation is better than an important call returned by a third party, or not returned at all.

I have dozens of conversations every day on the telephone, and the average length is two minutes. I'm able to pass messages, confront problems, and maintain friendships, all without fear that a third, fourth, or fifth party was misinterpreting the communication meant for me or from me.

In truth, most people can handle their personal messages in twenty minutes a day. But phone calls aren't the only medium. Quick notes, written in your own hand, also register on the appreciation scale. Former President George Bush was the master of handwritten notes. He wrote them often, sometimes as many as two dozen in a sitting, entirely in longhand. They weren't just to Cabinet members and heads of state, but to his secretaries, his Secret Service guards, and to ordinary citizens who had gotten his attention.

You have to be careful, however, not to devalue the currency. When I became a minority owner of the Atlanta Falcons, I made it a point not to send our head coaches a note after every victory, only after the big ones. This practice helped establish expectations—victories we counted on—and define exceptional achievements—victories we weren't supposed to have.

Today anyone who gets a call, a note, or a quick visit from me knows two things: one, that I care enough to follow their activities; and two, that I am aware of it when they have done the exceptional.

One of the most common frustrations of employees is not being recognized for hard (or smart) work. They fear their accomplishments are being obscured by others who want to take credit, or who at least want to see that they get none.

The personal message is tangible evidence for them that their exceptional work has been attributed to the right person. That knowledge by itself will spur most people on to more and greater achievements. But remember, it has to be individualized, from you to him or her. You can't mass mail a personal note.

MAKE LIFE A FRIENDLY GAME

If you have chosen to surround yourself with business tigers, you need to be ready to handle their adventurousness. Because you have given them the two prerequisites for surviving in the jungle—information and autonomy—they now have the freedom to act, including the great American freedom to fail.

If you try grand things, as tigers do, you sometimes fail grandly. How you respond to that failure determines whether they learn anything from it or forever after fear it. It will determine whether they ever again have the courage of grand aspirations and the capacity for grand achievements.

Instead of condemnation or derision, just ask: "What have you learned?"

One thing about tigers—and friends—is that they do not, so to speak, eat their young. They don't discard relationships because of a disappointment. They don't grow icy after a failure. And they don't let conventional rules of business thwart a relationship.

I recall early on at MSA, we spent two years struggling for cash. One of the friendships I struck up was with Larry Welke, the president of International Computer Programs, Inc. (ICP), the first publisher of software magazines and directories back in the late '60s. Operating with little money himself in those early days, Larry agreed to carry some of our advertising on the promise that we would work toward becoming a paying customer.

A lot of bottom-line hardliners would have balked at that, but Larry and I were able to communicate on a level that transcended business and became friendship. The relationship paid off for MSA in that it got us some business that helped keep us afloat in those rebuilding days. And later it paid off for ICP in that MSA became its biggest paying advertiser, and remained so for fourteen consecutive years.

The most eloquent tribute to friendship I've ever read came from the late Bobby Jones, the immortal golfer. The date was October 9, 1958; the place, an auditorium called Younger Graduation Hall, St. Andrews, Scotland. Jones, then hobbled by a debilitating spinal problem, had once been the quintessential Ugly American in Scotland. In a tantrum after being foiled by the Old Course's capricious winds, he'd thrown down his clubs and walked off the course, a failure.

But the people of St. Andrews didn't write him off. When he returned in 1927, his temper in rein, he emerged a hero, winning the British Open Championship on the Old Course.

Thirty-one years later—twenty-eight years after he had retired from the sport—he was back at the Old Course, confined to a wheelchair, to receive an award called the Freeman of the City and the Royal Borough of St. Andrews. His friends, who had long ago forgiven his pique, had not forgotten him. He was only the second American to receive this honor. The first had been a gentleman of some accomplishment named Benjamin Franklin, some 199 years earlier.

Jones spoke without notes, recounting with humor many of the times the Old Course had beaten him, dwelling little on his victories over it. But it was his passionate description of what his relationships with the people of St. Andrews had meant to him—friendships that began in his business, the business of golf, then flourished in the years after it—that most moved the people there, as well as those who read the words thereafter. He took the idea of friendships beyond people, beyond sport, and beyond business.

"There are two very important words in the English language that are very much misused and abused. They are 'friend' and 'friendship.' When I say to a person, 'I am your friend,' I have said about the ultimate."

The most touching moment in Jones's speech came when he said, "I could take out of my life everything except my experiences at St. Andrews, and I would still have had a rich and full life."

It would be nice, at the end of the day, to have friendships that meant as much. In 1992, when I retired from the active chairmanship of Dun & Bradstreet Software, I was able to stand in front of fifteen hundred people—mostly ex-MSAers, all friends—and repeat Bob Jones's words. The response from people afterward was a piquant confirmation that however you spend your life, the only people to spend it with are friends.

DO THE RIGHT THING

Every relationship gets tested. Children test their parents, employees test their managers, husbands test their wives (and, heaven knows, vice versa). No exceptions. So if you make the switch to relationship-based management, you will inevitably find yourself thinking about new boundaries. All of which will beg the question: How far should I go for this relationship?

It's true that relationships are in the details, but some of those details are larger than others. Whatever their dimension, you handle them all the same way: You do the right thing.

How do you determine the right thing? You just know.

An employee of mine, Lawrence Catchpole, once came to me with a tragic dilemma. His thirty-two-year-old wife, Jackie, had been diagnosed with a particularly virulent form of breast cancer. The young mother was told that the only treatment that presented any realistic chance for hope was a specialized bone marrow transplant, a procedure costing $150,000. Without it she had only a few months left.

But when Lawrence presented the insurance company with the diagnosis and recommendation, the agents said they wouldn't pay it on the grounds that the treatment was still "experimental"—in spite of the fact that it had been used around the country with considerable success.

When he related the story to me, I blew my top for one of the few times I can remember. I called the president of the insurance company—a company we'd paid millions in premiums to, a company that covered "cancer treatments" and "bone marrow transplants," but wouldn't cover bone marrow transplants for breast cancer—and read him the riot act. He wouldn't budge. I told him we'd see him in court.

Then I called Lawrence in and said, "First things first. Call your doctor and order the surgery as soon as possible. We'll pay the bill, then fight with the insurance company later." Jackie Catchpole had the surgery a few days later. (We did subsequently settle with the insurance company, collecting only half of the bill.)

The procedure sent the cancer into remission, giving Jackie over two more years with her family. (The disease did eventually spread, however, and finally claimed her in 1993.)

Was this the right thing to do? I can only say it was for me and for the culture of the company. Clearly not every company would make the same decision. Resources enter into the equation. But if you operate by the maxim that, "You can do what you can do," you don't have to look hard for the "right thing."

A good friend of mine in the software business, John Maguire, started a software company in Reston, Virginia, called Software AG of North America. In the mid '70s its only product was a complex software package called Adabas, a database management system. Early versions of the software were buggy (if promising), so Maguire brought in from Germany the man who had designed Adabas to try to handle the problems until the system could be refined.

The fellow worked tirelessly, often eighteen and twenty hours per day, reworking the software and taking help-line calls from customers with problems. He literally was the only person who knew the software's intricacies at that time, so his effort was the difference in the product's—and the company's—eventual success (both became the industry leaders). One day, on a whim, he went home for lunch. A small airplane lost power and crashed into the house, killing him instantly, and leaving his young daughter.

At that point, Software AG was large enough, and the product refined enough, that others could take over. But Maguire, remembering how his friend had almost single-handedly saved Software AG, diverted a portion of the company's funds to the care and college education of the daughter. It wasn't, in the scope of things, a massive investment for a multimillion-dollar enterprise—but it was exactly what the man would have requested.

Doing the right thing sometimes has limitations. It comes down, finally, to resources, imagination, and will. And if you have the last two, sometimes you need less of the resources, even for the grander gestures a relationship sometimes demands.

NOTHING ENDURES LIKE JUNGLE LOYALTY

There is nothing like an unmitigated disaster to test one of the jungle's most vital elements, which is loyalty. In good relationships, loyalty is given and expected. If you've built a business on a foundation of relationships, loyalty can get most people through the darkest of times.

I say this as an entrepreneur who came of age in an era when loyalty seemed to fall from fashion. It was an era of free-agent athletes, acquire-and-decimate mergers, and spiraling divorce rates—much like today. Everywhere you looked, fidelity was gone. But looking back, our ability at MSA to give and get loyalty was central to our success.

One anecdote about loyalty I often shared with MSA's people dealt with a crisis that erupted back when I was a young salesman with Honeywell. We had an account with a chicken feed processing outfit. To make a technical story short, the engineer who set up the computer made a terrible error. All of this chicken feed was processed incorrectly, then sent to the distributor. Suddenly we got the word: Chickens all over the United States were dying because the computer had mixed the feed wrong!

While I was horrified at what had happened, the bigger problem remained of correcting things fast. Instead of screaming for the engineer's head, I kept my loyalty and my cool intact. I called a fellow named Twon Chu, who was Honeywell's chief of engineering, and flew him in from Boston. He arrived ready to be defensive. But instead of attacking, I went out of my way to build him up and reassure him that we had every confidence in his ability (which truly was vast). He ended up bending over backward to correct things in a fraction of the time it might otherwise have taken. The main reason was because of the loyalty I showed him in a trying moment. It was a great lesson.

Then, of course, we had to deal with the chicken feed processor. My main contact was a man named Bill Glover, a great fellow with whom I'd cultivated an excellent relationship. Would this incident undo it? My boss at Honeywell said, "John, you've got to take care of Glover."

I told him, "Don't worry. I'm having him over for steaks this weekend."

He got there for what I was certain would be a perfect opportunity to allow me to patch up his concerns. Instead, my son Scott got sick and threw up on him, my dog bit him, and I burned the steaks.

In the face of all the disasters, Glover maintained his loyalty to me. We kept the account.

Loyalty doesn't always have to be demonstrated in a disaster. After I'd become friends with Fran Tarkenton in MSA's early days, I'd laughingly say things such as, "Fran, I'm your biggest fan."

He'd say wearily, "Right, Imlay." He'd heard that before.

One day when he was quarterbacking with Minnesota, the Vikings were playing the Chicago Bears at Soldier Field in Chicago. A freezing wind was blowing into the stadium off Lake Michigan. It was in the fourth quarter of the last game of the season. The Vikings were up by about three touchdowns and even the Bears' fans, among the sturdiest anywhere, were leaving to seek warmth.

Suddenly Tarkenton turns around and peers into the emptying seats. There I was, still in my seat behind the Vikings' bench, with a parka over my head, and shivering exactly like a Georgian in Chicago in winter.

Tarkenton just smiled and waved and shook his head. We're friends to this day. That's the best thing that loyalty can produce from any relationship.

JUNGLE RULE SUMMARY

BUILD A FRONT PORCH ON YOUR TREEHOUSE.

Be sure your business is set up to interact with people.

RELATIONSHIPS ARE IN THE DETAILS

Remember the little things.

MAKE IT PERSONAL

Whenever you can, make your interaction personal.

MAKE LIFE A FRIENDLY GAME

It really is okay to hire and do business with friends.

DO THE RIGHT THING

The right thing isn't always in the company handbook.

NOTHING ENDURES LIKE JUNGLE LOYALTY

Loyalty is the backbone of any relationship.

12

COMMUNICATING IN THE JUNGLE

Jungle Rule #12:
Tigers need only a scent to set them on
the hunt.

If brevity is the soul of wit, it is also the heart of business communications, and for the same reasons. The U.S. Constitution is about 3,000 words long. Lincoln's Gettysburg Address is about 260 words. The Lord's Prayer is under a hundred. Meanwhile, a Department of Agriculture report on the marketing of lettuce is more than 29,000 words.

Truly important thoughts usually don't require verbal marathons to relate. Just as vital things such as goals should be stated in a simple sentence, most business communications should follow the same path. You need only provide the merest scent to set your business tigers on the hunt.

Communicating in the jungle, as a rule, should be done both often and briefly. Once employees and customers know the general landscape (of the company, the industry, the product line, the strategy, and so on), communicating becomes a matter of stimulants instead of expositions.

Reinforce.

Few people want, need, or have time for lengthy discourses every day, even if they are from the boss and are generally positive. Business tigers in particular are bad candidates for management by lecture. Getting a job done is what drives them. They don't need to be told and retold how to do it. And if someone is getting the job done, it's bad business to divert him or her, even for excessive praise.

Doug MacIntyre, who started out in sales with MSA and rose to sales management, used to hand out small yellow business cards that said "Attatiger" on them. People loved them. One word reinforcements that said, in effect, "You're doing it right and we know it. Keep it up."

Head off.

Just as you can briefly reinforce what's working, you can, just as briefly, discourage what's not. It doesn't usually take a long-winded diatribe to correct most people, especially business tigers. In the case of the latter, you are dealing with a tremendous amount of energy. The challenge isn't to restrain that energy, but to rechannel it—to nudge it toward what works.

I've never had a problem calling someone aside and saying, "Look, we've tried our dead-level best and it just didn't work." No speeches, no point-by-point dissections of tactics, no thundering assaults. In a word, the people you want to surround yourself with are "nudgeable." They are open to changing plans and tactics because they want to succeed, so time-consuming lectures are unnecessary for them. A few words will do. If someone isn't nudgeable, that's another problem.

Enliven.

Anyone can make a point, but great communicators make them stick. One way they do this is by keeping the messages lively— which is also a great way to keep the message receivers lively. If you're giving speeches, make them visual, using film, slides, or props. Make them aural. Add music and other sound effects. Keep the speech well paced. Don't dwell on statistics, even in a shareholders meeting. They can get all the detail they want from the annual reports. At the meeting, they want confidence, honesty, and clarity. And they want to know: "Am I making money, and why or why not?"

Communicating in the jungle is no different from doing it anywhere else. If you respect your audience, whether it is one or 10,000, whether it is your banker or your customer, you can only conclude that brevity is the best way to show it. You've displayed respect for their time, which usually is short; respect for their intelligence, which ideally is high; and respect for your relationship, which shouldn't need endless polemics to be strong.

BEATING THE JUNGLE DRUMS

One of the enduring myths of business is that the press is predatory. A businessman once told me, "They get a lot more joy out of helping us fail than seeing that we succeed." There are two key words there that give away the mindset of the paranoid press-watcher: "... *helping* us fail" and "... *seeing* that we succeed."

It's just not the media's job to "help" us or to "see" that we do anything, except possibly tell the truth about public matters. It *is* the media's job to report a story accurately, fairly, and honestly.

Not all of them do it. Some don't check facts, some fabricate quotes, and some let their subjective views color a story. Some think that the only good journalism is negative journalism. Some are more interested in seeing their name in print than the truth. And some just don't like the way you said, *"No comment."*

But most members of the media are honest. They are reasonably meticulous, given the problems of deadlines, incomplete information, and sources that hedge, distort, and lie to them. They regret errors more than we give them credit for. And if you work with them instead of against them you can usually expect a fair story. Not puffery, just fairness.

The question of working with the media comes down to a few simple guidelines.

Work with the media.

Even if you don't talk to the members of the media (as Wal-Mart founder Sam Walton politely refused to do to the grave), at least don't show them disrespect. Don't spray-paint their camera lens or knock tape recorders from reporters' hands. Don't curse them, even those who try to bait you. Don't tell them, "Get a life." If you don't want to say anything, just say, "Thanks, I have nothing to say."

My advice, however, is to take time to work with them. Often the only balance to a story is what you have to say.

I always take the media's calls—in good times, bad times, and at all stops in between. If I'm not in, I return the calls that day, if possible. I speak with them evenings, weekends, and holidays because their deadlines sometimes demand that. If they need more information than I have, I show them where to get it. I have a job, and they have a job. If you respect the imperfections of the relationship, you can minimize the pain they cause. And in the long run, my company and I are better off for doing so.

Share their goals.

The eternal rule. If you understand what motivates the media— usually a balanced story—try to help them reach that goal (within reason). You need to answer their questions as honestly as you possibly can.

Be brief but quotable.

Learn how to speak with the media. It takes three things: honesty, conciseness, and color. Usually the media aren't looking for streams-of-consciousness answers—windy, rambling, overdetailed explanations to simple questions. That's pointless, exasperating, and requires so much note taking that the chances for misquotation and misinterpretation grow exponentially. What's preferable is the short, honest answer, quotably packaged.

Tolerate the exceptions.

You can never really tell beforehand what the media will seize on to hook its audiences. Sometimes it will be substance, other times nonsense. Once when I spoke before a distinguished gathering of managing directors and other British luminaries—including royalty—in London, I told a story about Japan to illustrate its competitive threat. I used a prop, a samurai sword, in telling the story. The next day, a London tabloid had a photograph of me on the front page holding the sword aloft. The caption read: "American Businessman Threatens Prince."

An Atlanta magazine ran an in-depth article on MSA and its resurgence. But in calling around, the writer had spoken with Fran Tarkenton, who mentioned our golfing. "He has the worst body I've ever seen," he said of me. "Yet he can still beat me, a pro athlete, in a game of golf." So, of course, the headline of this corporate profile read: "Worst Body!"

These things are going to happen. Don't let them turn you off.

Know your enemies, know your friends.

Clearly, this is one of life's good general habits. In dealing with the media, it's essential. When I say "enemies," I'm talking about the rare (sadly not extinct) bird who never lets a fact interfere with his preconceived opinion. My advice is to deal with him honestly, even if he doesn't do so with you. If you say, "No comment," he'll just huff away and write an "opinion piece" that supposes out loud why you aren't talking. Talk to these people. Be honest. Be brief in your responses. Direct them to anyone who can help them. Be as courteous as possible.

When I say "friends," I don't mean someone who is given to puffery. I'm really talking about journalists who are ritually fair and honest. That's as close to "friendship" as you are likely to get in media relationships—and probably as much as you should seek.

In 1985, MSA sold off an acquisition that had failed to work. The acquisition of this small personal computer software company, Peachtree Software, in 1981 had been a very high-profile move for us. Four years later, it was clear we had underestimated the difficulties of the deal and decided to spin it off.

The media in large part lined up the artillery and began taking potshots at us over the failure. It was the only time I'd ever really felt ganged up on. The editor for *Datamation Magazine*, one of the most respected journals in computing since the 1950s, called us up when we were feeling pretty down and out. She had no preconceived storyline; she just wanted to know what had happened.

The editor—Becky Barna—wrote a story that explained honestly not only what happened that caused the acquisition to fail, but why we had gotten such a broadside of tough publicity.

The answer to the latter was simple: We'd played some pretty loud trumpets in making the acquisition; the bad rap was the echo coming back. We'd made ourselves highly visible. As Ms. Barna wrote (quoting me) in the article, "The higher up the flagpole the monkey climbs, the more of his ass you can see."

In good times or bad, that kind of visibility needs a "friend."

If you have established relationships with the media that cover you—if they know they can call you and get a truthful answer—you can usually take the wind out of badly conceived or poorly researched stories. McCormack & Dodge, our archrivals for many years, was particularly adept at planting sky-is-falling stories—this or that product line was in trouble, a financial crisis was looming, and so on. When a reporter called to say that M & D had said this or that about us, I would just laugh and reply disparagingly, "Consider the source." Those three words always put a cloud over the heads of the critics and led to more thorough research by the writer. And thorough research is, in the end, all you can ask of the media.

IF IT'S WORTH DOING, IT'S WORTH FLAIR

Communicating in the jungle takes flair: class, style, imagination, drama, humor. In MSA's early days, it wasn't difficult to stand out as a software company. There were a couple of hundred companies at the most. By the mid 1980s, there were 20,000 software products available from 5,000 companies in America alone. In a jungle that crowded, flair will separate you from the pack.

In 1981, we calculated that small personal computers were going to replace some of the larger and more expensive minicomputers that many businesses used for their information processing. MSA had just gotten into the personal computer software market, and we wanted to make a point about where we thought the industry was going.

At first, we considered just preparing a press kit describing our strategy in PC software. But that wouldn't make a strong enough statement. People might miss the significance of the strategy. Then we were going to elaborate on why the minicomputer industry was in its death throes.

"Death? Wait a minute! Let's *announce* the death of the mini!"

"Great! How should we announce it?"

"I know—let's have a funeral!"

"We'll put a minicomputer into a casket! Imlay can deliver a eulogy!"

"Fantastic! Let's have the casket carried into the conference, led by a New Orleans jazz band!"

"Perfect!"

MSA's PR meetings tended to be a lot like the old Mickey Rooney–Judy Garland musicals: "I got it! Let's put on a show!"

It was a long way from a press kit. The "funeral" got coverage, with photographs, in every computer journal and in a range of mainstream media. The personal computer software division got off to a fast start, the press had its angle (and color), and millions of potential clients had a perfectly clear picture of MSA's strategy. It was a great funeral.

Early in my sales career, Honeywell came out with some new equipment called key-to-tape machines. They represented a big advance over IBM's old keypunch equipment for data entry. I wanted to get the attention of the world and tell them IBM's offering was outdated.

Showtime.

I told Russ Henderson, my boss, what I had in mind. He liked flair, but some stunts made him edgy. He left town so that if some-one complained, he could at least say he wasn't involved.

After he left, I rented a big hall and had customers and media brought in by buses. After spending a bit of time characterizing the future as one in which these new machines would be indispensable, I rolled an old IBM keypunch machine onto the stage. Then I took a baseball bat and beat the blue out of Big Blue. The crowd roared. The point was made.

IBM was incensed. Meanwhile, Russ was saying, "Hey, I was in Boston when Imlay did that."

Flair can sometimes get you noticed in the jungle in ways you hadn't counted on. We once had this big product rollout and invited every news organization and writer whose name we'd ever gathered to see the debut. It was a fairly elaborate show. I went through sev-eral costume changes—including a business suit, a tuxedo, and a lion tamer's outfit (the tiger I brought on stage didn't seem to mind)—and we ended up with the coverage we had anticipated from industry journals.

A couple of months later, I got a call from an Associated Press reporter. He wanted to know my reaction to being selected as "America's Best-Dressed Businessman" by an organization called the Fashion Foundation of America. At first, I thought it was some kind of joke, so I asked for his AP number and called him right back. It was legitimate. Apparently, we had included in our media list some fashion reporters who ended up being quite taken with my several outfits. I was in some fantastic company with that year's selection—Michael Jackson, Frank Sinatra, Ronald Reagan . . . and me. I said, "They must have needed a token slob."

But carpe diem. I confess, the most productive cow in history never got milked the way I did this one. I was even covered in Mos-cow's papers.

There are several serious ironies here. One is that I buy all my suits off the rack. I don't buy from the fashion designers; I buy at a store called Zachary's, from the same guy I've been going to for thirty years.

The reason I go to him is because, as a trainee salesman with

Univac, I had one suit—a $4.99 seersucker job—and was voted (deservedly) worst-dressed guy in my sales training class. Desperate, I went to one fashionable shop, asked for credit, and was turned down. I went across the street to Zachary's, and the sales manager took a chance on me. Now, suddenly, he had outfitted "America's Best-Dressed Businessman" and done it right off the rack. The final irony is that, because I am colorblind, I don't even pick out my clothes; my wife, Geri, does.

For years afterward, whenever I was speaking somewhere, I would have the person introducing me mention my selection to the best-dressed list. Then I would come out and say, "It didn't change me at all." Then I'd pull my hand from my pocket, wearing on it a sequined glove.

Flair, besides being useful, is some great fun.

MAKE TRACKS

One piece of advice that comes up a lot for today's businesspersons is: Get out of the den. Make tracks. Circulate. Meet people. Get involved. Tell your story. Work for your industry. The worst management suite in the world is the ivory tower.

When you get out into the world, it's a good idea to have communication on your mind—communicating with prospective clients, with industry peers, with the media, with lawmakers, with the financial community. That's how the world finds out about you, and learns what sets you apart.

If you're brave enough to be leading a charge with a business of some kind, you need to have the fortitude to tell people your ideas. You don't have to be a Churchillian orator to pull this off. But you have to have the ideas; you have to find the forums; and you have to get involved. Making tracks is the source of a whole new world of relationships.

Early in my career with MSA, I got involved with an organization called ADAPSO, the Association of Data Processing Service Organizations. In the beginning, ADAPSO didn't want much to do with software companies. Its membership was mostly service bureaus, and they tended to regard software products as a kind of aberration.

But all that changed. The software industry came of age right alongside MSA, and today it has more members in the ITAA (ADAPSO's new name) than any other industry segment. Other MSA people joined me in getting involved on ADAPSO's executive committee and with its semiannual conferences. We became activists. We conducted conference sessions on industry topics such as financing, software piracy, IBM's competitive behavior, Japan's threat to U.S. technology, the industry's image, and a range of technologies.

Because we got out and got involved—and did it with passion—MSA's image was elevated among peers, with Wall Street, and with the world's information consumers. We rarely talked about MSA's products or anything that conspicuously self-serving. Our efforts were to communicate our views on industry issues that affected all of the companies.

By taking a leadership role there, we established a bond with our peers—including our competitors—that a reclusive company would never find. Even better, we were able (in concert with other activists) to effect changes in business practices that had a positive effect on ADAPSO's members.

All of that activity in communicating, done with passion, leads to even better opportunities. I eventually had the honor of becoming chairman of ADAPSO—the group that once kept software companies in a corner—and, subsequently, of leading its Image Committee for several years. When the ADAPSO Foundation was formed to bring computers and technology to handicapped and underprivileged children, I had the opportunity to work on its behalf.

In 1983, thanks in part to the exposure I'd received with ADAPSO, I became the first software company executive to deliver the keynote address to the National Computer Conference in Anaheim, California. At a hundred thousand people, it was then the largest industry gathering anywhere. I spoke before almost ten thousand of them for the keynote address. We used a huge screen to beam in Senator Frank Lautenberg, a New Jersey Democrat who, before becoming a U.S. senator, had been chairman of Automatic Data Processing, one of America's largest computer services firms. I coined a term that day—the "chief information officer," or CIO—which has since become part of the industry lexicon.

What did making all of these tracks accomplish for MSA? It went well beyond the exposure of the moment. By venturing out into this region of the jungle, I met a world of new people. I met the executives of a number of companies that MSA would later acquire. I met the fellow who would guide MSA's public offering. I met the media I would work with on hundreds of stories. I met dozens of people who would eventually work for us. And I met the fellow who would finally buy the company.

So I have an inveterate belief in getting out and communicating. It comes back again to people and relationships. I detest the word "networking," which is essentially the collecting of business cards at cocktail parties. If you're out of that ivory tower, communicating and involved, you don't have to "network." You'll have relationships of substance. And those are what will see you through the jungle.

JUNGLE RULE SUMMARY

TIGERS NEED ONLY A SCENT TO SET THEM ON THE HUNT.

Avoid windy lectures; tigers are nudgeable.

BEATING THE JUNGLE DRUMS

Work with the media, not with the myth.

IF IT'S WORTH DOING, IT'S WORTH FLAIR

A little class, style, and imagination never hurt an idea.

MAKE TRACKS

Get out of the ivory tower and start communicating with the world.

13

LET THE TIGERS RUN

Jungle Rule #13:
Give your permission not to seek your
permission.

This rule really is about cultivating freedom. And about using forgiveness as a management tool.

Immutable Jungle Fact: If you grant autonomy, you also have
to grant indulgences to the people you've made autonomous. You
have to let them run. If you've empowered people to make decisions, the right people will make good ones most of the time. But
from time to time, everyone screws up. Or they make decisions with
widespread implications. You can't let these incidents become
showstoppers.

Think for a minute about unencumbered doers. Bill Gates
comes to mind. Gates, chairman of Microsoft Corporation,
worked closely with IBM to build a $500 million company. But
then he saw that there would be no more quantum leaps working
hand in hand with IBM, because Big Blue moved in so much
slower motion than he and Microsoft. So, at considerable risk, he
arbitrarily decided to compete against the very company he had

ridden to success—and at this writing has a company with a valuation of $25 billion. By all, save IBM, he's been forgiven.

After you've prepared your business tigers, you turn them loose. You've given them responsibility. You've encouraged their initiative. You've freed their imagination. You've given them license to prowl, to stalk, to make something happen. Just the sheer amount of pure *activity* these freedoms spawn assures that, sooner or later, the tiger will end up in a snare. It's up to you to free him.

One of the places autonomy can cause conflict for tigers is in the sale. It's here that goals are identified and shared, that extra resources are committed to reach them—and that lines sometimes are crossed.

As a young salesman, I used to annoy my boss because I would breach convention to get a sale or keep a promise. On the one hand, he would tell me he was pleased with how I was taking care of my customers. On the other hand, he would add, his job was "to make a profit, John." Sometimes these two elements clashed.

For example, computers can be strangely dependent creatures. They often need certain types of software in order to make them run as fast or as well as advertised. When I would find a customer who needed one of these catalyst packages, I would try to convince my boss to throw it in so that we could deliver on our promise. If the economics weren't right, he would go to the mat with me.

If I couldn't convince him, I'd go out and buy it myself. He would shake his head, but he always forgave me. And I knew that he always would. That made a world of difference in how creative I could be in solving customer problems.

Dipping into my commission to pay for some necessary complementary software is an extreme example, but the principle is universal. Customers simply are not all the same. Their situations vary, their management resources vary, their budgets vary, their technical people vary, their goals vary. They are dissimilar in far more ways than they are alike. The result is that you have to be flexible in devising solutions from customer to customer, even when the core product you sell them is identical.

This has held true for me for more than three decades in sales.

Having the freedom to take necessary actions in dissimilar situations has made literally millions of dollars of difference. While it was sometimes creative, sometimes touching the boundaries of policy and even acceptability, sometimes driving good bosses up the wall, I usually didn't cross the line. Nor, usually, did the people I later empowered with freedom of their own.

Fortunately for me, I usually had bosses who understood the value of autonomy. Consequently, they also understood forgiveness as a management tool. I'd also had managers (never for long) who, with their lockstep mentality and blind fidelity to tepid convention, completely destroyed initiative in people. It was like being encased in concrete. You might as well hire and program robots—which is already being done through computerized solicitations—if you're going to bypass one of the greatest qualities human beings possess.

In the business jungle, as in the bush, tigers are eventually freed to leave their families. If they're to survive, they need every asset possible. The facility and freedom to take actions, to imagine solutions on the fly, to reasonably commit themselves and their companies, are all part of the tiger persona and are fundamental to their success. You have to keep moving, keep prowling, keep attacking, and freedom is a marvelous animator. As Will Rogers used to say, "Even if you're on the right track, you'll get run over if you just sit there."

EVEN TIGERS NEED BOUNDARIES

The natural question is: If you've freed the tigers to run, who keeps them from running away?

Any time you choose to manage by empowering people, you have an obligation to back off and let them operate. You can't pretend to be the great tiger liberator and then proceed to covertly manipulate them. But as stockholders and bosses are apt to remind you, a business has to make a profit, lest it become like the government.

Even though most business tigers know and respect their limitations, sometimes passion, well intentioned as it might be, edges them past the boundaries. Thus even the most free-spirited business needs checks and balances, mostly so the checks don't bounce and the balances don't fall.

In deal making at MSA, we decided effectively to package our checks and balances in some technical wizards who also knew sales contracts. One of them was Harry Howard, a senior software technician who joined MSA smack in the middle of the company's worst crisis year. He had developed a resounding sense of what excesses could do to a company. That insight became even more valuable when he decided to make the unusual move into contracts evaluation, deciding which deals could fly and which were grounded.

While he understood the unusual latitude people had in MSA's jungleselling, we knew he was exactly the tiger who could patrol the outermost boundaries—the ones that encompassed great latitude and imagination, but wouldn't hurt the company. On those occasions when someone slipped past the boundaries, he would spring.

But only as a last resort.

First, he was an analyst. He would do everything he could to answer customer questions, solve problems, and bring deals to fruition. His job was to *make the sale happen*. But first he had to know exactly what was going on.

As a senior software technician sitting in on a sales closing (strange bedfellows, but effective), his first priority was to see if anything in the deal exceeded the boundaries. Were we committing too many technical people? For too long a time? Were there conflicts with other implementations? Were there remote sites that would be too expensive to support? Had we offered too costly a discount on complementary products? Had we committed to too aggressive an implementation schedule? The mix could be extremely complicated.

His second priority was to be a problem solver. If something went over the line, he was to see if he could *extend the boundaries to encompass it*. Could resources be shifted? Could the schedule be changed? What was the long-term advantage of a short-term loss?

His third priority was to nix any deals that were just bad business. He was so good at the first two that the third rarely got exercised in all the years he had sentry duty.

For MSA, most creative deal making took the form of technical commitments from us to help get a company's accounting or financial operation up to speed, and sometimes radically overhauled. Our primary software products were major financial and accounting systems that were at the core of a business's operations. So they always affected a lot of people, computers, reports, and management information. And they often meant big changes for our customers—changes that we felt obligated to support materially, technically, and informationally.

Again, we learned early on that we weren't just "selling software," but *solving business problems,* which is much more complex. Thus our people needed the freedom to take initiatives that got to the heart of a solution, not just a sale.

It's ultimately important to have an arbiter prowling the perimeters of commitments. After all, there are two businesses at stake here—yours and the customer's—with all that implies. But make sure that your monitors are creative problem solvers themselves.

If they aren't, and they spend all their time shooting holes in the special aspects of a deal, they'll kill the deals—not to mention the initiative of the deal makers. But if they know their job is to look at devising solutions—whistles, bells, and eccentricities, commonplace and unique, major and minor—and then to somehow *make that deal happen,* more often than not the deal *will* happen.

THINK GRAND THEMES

MSA always encouraged people to think grand. Whether it was in selling or hosting conferences or attacking markets, the act of thinking grand was habit forming. If you knew you had the license to do it—the *charge* to do it—then after a while you just consulted another part of your brain when concocting ideas. You bypassed the soft, safe, doughy notions. No more tepid speakers for meetings.

No more pastel logos. You sound your barbaric yawp over the rooftops of the world, as Walt Whitman would have it. And people will remember.

Eventually, thinking grand themes becomes part of the corporate culture. When it does, it becomes a kind of perpetual challenge. You get a reputation for treating people to the extraordinary, and to some extent that's difficult to continually improve upon. If you had a moving speech by a famous person at a meeting, you're expected next time to have a more gripping one by a more famous person. And so it goes, on and on.

Conversely, it's progressively easier to entice people to attend your functions because they *have* high expectations. And once you get them into the den with grander themes, you can cultivate the relationships with the less glittery (but ultimately more important) ones, the themes such as service, empathy, quality, passion, and knowledge. Which is where you want grand themes eventually to lead.

And grand themes don't have to break the bank, if you use a little imagination. Everyone else is shooting off fireworks at their meeting? You arrange for a picnic across from a space shuttle lift-off. Everyone else is passing out new pen sets to salespersons at the annual kickoff? You rent a live tiger and walk it among them. Everyone else debuts their ad campaign with the theme of "Race to the Top"? You take them to the Indianapolis Motor Speedway and have them photographed in a race car. Everyone else lights their Olympic flames with a torch? You use an archer with a flaming arrow.

Think grand themes, then bring them to life. When we devised the theme "You have to be a tiger to survive in '75," we were mulling ideas on how to present it. The first time it was suggested that we bring a *live* tiger to a sales kickoff meeting, people were taken aback. But then we began asking that wondrously critical question: "But why *can't* we?"

The next thing you know, we were trying to bring a crazy idea to life. You start making calls. You ask questions. You find out the costs, the risks, the precautions. Suddenly, the idea isn't so crazy anymore.

Grand themes usually have long lives and spawn great subthemes that people can use in a lot of ways. If your theme is "Swim with the sharks," I suppose it's possible to bring a bass to the meeting and hope people identify with its struggle against the jaws of the world. But (and I say this from experience), it's better to bring the shark. There's very little in the way of subthemes you can do with a bass.

One note of caution: There must always be a logical tie-in to your grand theme. The object of this exercise is to make a lasting impression, to give people an image that they can draw inspiration from and talk about for perhaps six months or a year. So the image you choose must be related to the message you have.

There's an old adage: It costs just 20 percent more to go first class. The same could be said about grand themes. It takes about 20 percent more creativity—a zone too often untapped by most people—to pick the shark over the bass. And, of course, it takes the freedom to entertain crazy ideas.

Do you have it?

JUNGLE RULE SUMMARY

GIVE YOUR PERMISSION NOT TO SEEK YOUR PERMISSION.

Let the tigers run.

EVEN TIGERS NEED BOUNDARIES

But make sure the person guarding them is a problem solver.

THINK GRAND THEMES

The world will remember.

14

REMEMBER WHO YOU WORK FOR

Jungle Rule #14:
The king of the jungle is the customer.

The root of MSA's belief in sharing goals was that we knew our success was based on the success of our customers. Period. So one of our corporate missions was to make sure everyone knew who really was boss.

One of the world's most confused issues is who any of us works for. If you ask a statehouse worker who he works for and he replies, "the government," then you know what I mean. He doesn't work for the government; he works for the taxpayers. At least he's supposed to.

But it's that foggy understanding of who we're really in business to serve that screws up our goals, our priorities, and eventually, our results. A government worker who passionately believes he is in the service of the taxpayer has an entirely different view of things such as taxes, government spending, bureaucratic inefficiency, and ultimate results than someone who plods to the shop each day to "work for the government."

The same problem exists in business. In the vast majority of instances, you don't really work for the company that signs your pay-checks. You work for the customers who provide the money *for* those paychecks. Your company is just an organizational link to them. And those customers can dispense with that link—and you—whenever they become dissatisfied with what you've done.

MSA began with the theme of "People are the key," but we quickly added: *The customer is king.* There was no guessing about where we put our emphasis. We stressed that idea at every gather-ing of employees, every sales training session, every management meeting, and every customer encounter.

Like most messages we wanted to get across, we tried to bring it to life with imagery. At our annual user group conferences, we ac-tually would select a Customer of the Year, then crown him king (or her queen). We'd wrap him in a robe and give him a sceptre. Then the MSA executives on stage would kneel, head bowed—me included—with the instruction that we couldn't rise until the "king" ordered us to. One of them kept us kneeling for five long minutes, much to the delight of the audience of several thousand. But we couldn't have asked for a better moment to register the image. No one moved an inch. Point made.

Of course, the most important customer-is-king points are made in the trenches. The relationship between you and your cus-tomers is strengthened only by what you deliver, not what you promise. It goes back to the idea of finding out their goals and help-ing them achieve them, solving problems at midnight, involving them in important decisions (e.g., product strategy discussions, in-dustry direction conferences, new technology sessions, and so on), and demonstrating that you are, in fact, working for *them.*

And then every once in a while there is a magnolia blossom. MSA was hosting a customer shindig at the farm of Bonnie Brooks, a beautiful young singer who once even recorded an album for cus-tomers. The only thing missing at her farm was a magnolia tree, which happened to be what one of our customers wanted badly to see.

It happened that I had three huge seventy-year-old magnolia trees at my home, so we drove there to give the customer a look. He wanted a blossom, but saw they were well up in the tree. But the customer is king, right? So I hauled my creaky body over to the tree and climbed up it. It was one of those deals where halfway up you think something intelligent like: *I'm a CEO, and I have bark scratches on my thighs.*

I finally reached a blossom and then—naturally—slipped and came crashing down, blossom in hand. I gave it to the customer, then limped for days afterward. But it was worth it. By the next morning, thanks to this fellow with a magnolia blossom, the story was known to every customer at the party. The sales staff was repeating it as the quintessential customer-is-king folklore. The story still makes the rounds.

The scratches are gone.

OUTSERVICE THE COMPETITION

Quick tip for the jungle diner:

The sale is the cake, but service is the meat and potatoes.

In other words, the sale tastes great when it happens, but service is the heart of the meal. If you're in the business of selling your product, you might want to consider retirement. The business of selling your *company*—in the form of its service—is a lot more lucrative.

Competitors for years had a ball portraying MSA as a flashy marketing group—"But what do they *really* have?" The answer was inexhaustible customer service. Our sales strategies certainly encompassed the selling phase, but it was service that built the relationships.

Most companies have service departments, help lines, and even on-line, computer-assisted support for clients who want to do some high-tech rummaging for answers. But even those are becoming conventional.

Especially if your business is service driven, you need to consult with customers in every phase of your operation that affects them. Even when the discussion is one they don't particularly want to have, the idea of "customer service" demands that you talk to them, explore with them, have it out, whatever—all the things that happen in relationships.

In MSA's early days, we struggled mightily with cash flow problems. Some months we'd sell $2 million, other months nothing. If we were going to service customers the way we intended—which was by outservicing everyone else—we needed to have a source of cash flow that provided stability.

We devised what we called "maintenance fees," which was an annual charge to every customer. The fees would pay for research and development, ongoing product support, new versions of products—all the things that would help us service our customers better.

When I sent out letters inviting the customers to the meeting, I told them what the subject was—that is, that we wanted them to pay a yearly fee over and above the sum on their signed contracts. Twelve of them showed up with lawyers in tow.

The early part of the meeting had all of the civility of the Valentine's Day Massacre. But by the time I was able to explain MSA's extensive new concept of service—not just help lines, but strategic planning councils, development partnerships, user conferences—all twelve signed on.

It became a turning point in the history of the software industry. Today, the vast majority of companies use maintenance revenue to smooth out cash flow and to fund research, development, and service. For us, it's a $300 million–plus source of annual income and without question is the reason we can continue providing service at the level we do.

The lesson was a useful one on several counts. One was that customers are willing to pay for service, as long as it genuinely advances their business. Our whole story was that they weren't buying a "software product," but a whole company—one that would become an extension of their own business, their own R & D, their own information systems. That definition is extremely service-intensive.

Our basic principle of service, as Bill Graves used to say, was simple: *The success of MSA is dependent upon the success of the customer.* And service, not product, would determine that success. So in answer to all those competitors who kept asking, "But what do they *really* have?"—now they know.

And it is service that keeps people coming back. My all-time champion customer is a guy named Charlie Darnell, one of the crustiest scowlers ever to walk the planet. But he loves good service more than he cares for any product or any company. What a fantastic lesson he provides.

Charlie heads the data processing for a Georgia company called Lithonia Lighting. I sold him punched-card equipment in 1960, solid-state computers when I worked for Univac, Honeywell computers after that. He would change right along with me. The reason was because he knew I would treat any problem he had as if it was the only problem I had.

Then one day Lithonia hired a new technical manager, who proceeded to throw out my Honeywell computers and install IBM. I sued Lithonia Lighting for breach of contract. I won. The case, *Honeywell, Inc. v. Lithonia Lighting, Inc.*—which was heard by Judge Newell Edenfield, who later oversaw MSA's bankruptcy—provided a landmark decision. It basically held that computer leasing was a reality and leasing contracts were binding (we had a five-year contract). And it cost Lithonia $641,000.

Charlie might well have been perturbed enough by the lawsuit to forever after cease doing business with me, but he wasn't. The reason was service. He didn't hesitate a second to return to the fold. Later when I took over MSA, he used the IBM equipment because MSA sold IBM software. He joined MSA's highest customer advisory board—the Customer Council—which worked with MSA's executives on strategic technology planning. He's still on the Council today, thirty-three years after I sold him the punched-card machines. He never did really buy products.

It was service all along.

TRACK THE CUSTOMERS' MINDPRINTS

Doug MacIntyre was an MSA salesman—and later sales manager—who was fantastic at getting inside the minds of prospects and customers. He knew the Great Jungle Truth that, if the customer is telling you (by whatever means) what he wants, then listen. After all, you're working for him.

Normally, MacIntyre would use his intelligence and inquisitiveness to mine the little nuggets that gave him an edge in selling and problem solving. But he also knew that clients tell you in other ways—through people they work with, through past patterns of behavior, through speeches, through their background and education; anywhere they might leave "mindprints."

A few years ago, he was dead into a red-hot competition for an account called Byrd Press. It was an important strategic sale because the company was buying an entire line of systems. As often was the case, our chief rival in this was McCormack & Dodge. M & D was throwing around a pretty hefty discount, so MacIntyre began looking for mindprints to get an edge.

After some digging, he learned that the president of the company had written a book. It wasn't just any book, but one about what he saw as important in the corporation. This, MacIntyre knew, was like striking gold. He took it home and spent six hours reading—practically memorizing—every word. He highlighted everything in the book that was germane to his proposal.

Then he sat down and wrote an unsolicited proposal for the business, which was also something M & D hadn't done. In the executive summary of the proposal, he quoted—verbatim in some cases, paraphrasing in others—the executive's book. He did not attribute the quotes, but let them stand as examples of sound thinking, which they were.

MacIntyre knew that, even though he hadn't sent the proposal to the president/author (he was working with other people), eventually the guy would read it. A massive expenditure was involved and would require a high-level signoff. And he knew that the president could be the fox in the deal, the guy who would guide it through if he liked what he read.

"When I finally got to meet him," MacIntyre says, "he had the proposal lying on the table in front of him. He had taken a yellow highlighter and highlighted the points I had made that had agreed with his thinking in the book.

"He said, 'When I read this proposal, I instantly liked you because I like the way your company thinks.'

" 'You know,' he added, 'we could never establish this level of chemistry with your competition.' "

Macintyre says the book not only landed the sale, but it suggested a customer support strategy that only rarely was so precisely laid out. McCormack & Dodge never did learn where MacIntyre had gotten his edge in the sale. "They probably thought I had underbid them," he says, "but actually we were higher. I'm sure they thought we pulled some trick, but all we did was spend a little time reading the book. We outhustled them."

Finding the mindprints is essential for all levels of selling, and for good relationships in general. If you're operating under the premise that the king of the jungle is the customer, you have to know what he is thinking: what is important to him, how he measures success, and how he defines good relationships.

It's usually not laid out in so tidy a form as MacIntyre found, though sometimes it is. But if you're not looking for mindprints, you'll never find them.

GET OUT OF THE TIGER'S SKIN AND INTO THE CUSTOMER'S

One of the mistakes companies make is thinking they're selling the same product to every customer. In MSA's case, we learned that what was a vanilla accounting system to one customer was a management information system to another. It mattered little that we sold accounting software that embraced the same Generally Accepted Accounting Principles (GAAP) or operated with the same commands or utilized the same documentation.

Every customer still was different. Every customer had special problems. Every customer had unique goals. A commitment to that level of customized service—making each customer believe that his problems were the sole focus of our corporate energy—is a terrific way to distinguish yourself in a crowded jungle.

I've spoken earlier in this book about the tiger's need for versatility. It is vital in building this service culture. What you have to do is be willing to get into your customers' skins, to learn their businesses. That's the only way you get true empathy for their problems and goals.

Sometimes it's more of a challenge than others.

When I was a young computer salesman, I had a customer named Ed Elson. Ed was one of these brilliant guys who had great ideas but could be tough to do business with. He was an ironhard negotiator and didn't easily warm up to relationships. But I was committed to staying after him.

His father had had this idea that airports would be good places to have book concessions. Travelers were usually looking for something to read on or between flights, he'd observed, and maybe they would like something more than newspapers from a stand. Now Ed, following the lead, was opening up some bookstores and found a booming business, which soon needed computers to help it manage inventory, among other things. That's when I got the call.

At the time, there wasn't any software that could do what he needed to have done. It would have to be customized. The other problem was that I didn't know the first thing about the bookstore business. If I was going to service this guy, I was going to have to learn his business from scratch.

I rode the trucks, delivered magazines, studied distribution, talked to book and magazine accountants, and basically studied as if I was going into the business. After a while, we'd automated the whole operation.

Ed ended up becoming famous for his automation, and it was used as a model for other bookstores. His operation flourished. Eventually, he sold the stores to W.H. Smith & Company for $65 million. And, also eventually, he warmed up to the relationship. To-day he is the U.S. Ambassador to Denmark.

I was never sorry for the effort. The *project* had succeeded. That was the victory. And I figured if I could survive Ed—who later became an art collector and philanthropist—service for most people would be gravy.

It was.

JUNGLE RULE SUMMARY

THE KING OF THE JUNGLE IS THE CUSTOMER.

Remember who you work for.

OUTSERVICE THE COMPETITION

Where they give up, you're just starting.

TRACK THE CUSTOMERS' MINDPRINTS

When you know what they're thinking, you'll know how to win them.

GET OUT OF THE TIGER'S SKIN AND INTO THE CUSTOMER'S

Learn their business the way you learn your own.

15

LIONS, TIGERS, AND BEARS

Jungle Rule #15:
To convey a message that lives, get a symbol
that lives.

I can't wrap up Section 2 of *Jungle Rules* without a few words about the exotic animals that MSA became so well known for. The role they ended up having in the company wasn't planned. We brought in our first animal—a tiger—just to do something memorable. That the animals turned out to be so effective for communicating themes, inspiring ideas, immortalizing images, and motivating people was as surprising as their spontaneous behavior. Which reminds me: If you can't ad lib, find another symbol; this one isn't for you.

It all really began before MSA. Back in my days with Honeywell, my boss, Russ Henderson, used to call people "tiger." He had two purposes: one, the word connoted to him toughness, tenacity, and energy. Russ liked to spontaneously acknowledge people who had those qualities with a rousing slap on the back and a charge to "Go get 'em, tiger." And two, he couldn't remember everyone's name in an organization as large as Honeywell. By referring to people as "tiger," he could make his point spontaneously whenever he saw someone do something extraordinary or undertake something challenging.

Years later, after I'd joined MSA, I still was calling people "tiger" because I too liked what the word said. To me it meant strength, independence, grace, relentlessness, and intelligence—the traits of unconquerability. And, like Russ, I didn't always know everyone's name, especially after MSA began doubling in size every year. But even at that, there always was a reaction from them to being called "tiger." They really walked off a little more erect, a little more confident, maybe even a little more unconquerable.

At the beginning of 1975, we foresaw a tough year on the horizon because of the recession. We decided to use the theme: "You have to be a tiger to survive in '75." The word "tiger" already was part of the lore of the company, so taking it to the next step seemed logical. We knew we wanted a symbol that would be memorable. One that would have its nine lives; that we could later use in marketing, speeches, literature, videos—anywhere we wanted to revive the message.

But it all had to tie into an initial encounter that wouldn't be forgotten; one that could remotivate people every time they saw another image; one that would be so burned into people's minds that they would talk about it for months or even years (it turned out to be for decades). So I said:

"Let's get a live tiger and bring it to the sales kickoff."

After we got past the discussions of "But what if it eats our sales force?" we began exploring how you really get a live tiger into a hotel ballroom. It turned out to be not all that tricky. We decided not to tell anyone. We just dropped hints about the "surprise" and let people imagine what might be coming.

No one imagined it.

The day of the kickoff at the old Eastlake Country Club, we walked in with a Bengal tiger. Men stopped eating their hors d'oeuvres in mid chew. A few women shrieked. A waiter dropped a tray of Bloody Marys. People began edging toward the door. I thought: Well, they're not going to forget *this*.

After taking a few moments to explain that the tiger was harmless, I began to talk about the theme, what it really meant to be a tiger. Until then, it had been just another slogan, a string of words with a message but no depth. Nothing to really make it stand out among the world's clichés.

But suddenly, as the crowd began to edge back toward us, something remarkable happened. The cliché took on resonance. There was this magnificent beast, this creature that symbolized survival in the wild, living and breathing there among us—almost one of us. Nothing else on earth could have conveyed its strength, its dignity, its fearlessness, or its confidence.

It was as if all the years of referring to people as "tiger" suddenly came to fruition. *This is it. This is what we were talking about. This is what you sensed in yourselves when we called you that.*

I'd honestly only been looking for a memorable symbol, something unconventional, but the tiger turned out to mean much more to people. Later, they became almost mesmerized by it. They came up and petted its head or stroked its flanks. They posed for photographs with it. Twila Lowe, MSA's receptionist, wound up on the cover of our annual report, smiling broadly, arm around the tiger. Beauty and the beast. No more fear, just a special kinship.

For those who were there that day, the kinship still exists.

The tiger was perfect for our theme that year. It's vital, when you get into the exotic metaphors that create memorable messages, that you have a clear link from metaphor to message. You don't want to bring in an exciting animal just to parade it without making a point.

In 1981, we took MSA public. We wrestled for a while over the perfect symbol for this important event. We finally settled on the eagle. He would symbolize the theme: "Come fly with me." Ken Millen, MSA's director of human resources and its animal procurement guru, suggested taking the eagle all over the country to our various offices. At one point, we took the show up to Midwest Vice President Pete Morgan's Chicago office. The eagle took over from there.

Ken Millen:

The eagle had the most in-depth meaning for what was going on at MSA at the time. Its name was Sundance, and it came from a conservationist in Oregon. It had a wingspan of about six feet. I recall when we had it in Chicago, we took it outside during a break in the meeting. All these birds around it were going crazy, because this huge bird had invaded their space. But the eagle was oblivious to it all. It just stood there regally perched on the trainer's arm. It was a great image.

We went back inside and began the meeting again. Suddenly the eagle got agitated. At first we couldn't figure out why. Then we saw that he was looking out a window, and there was a squirrel about two football fields away.

It is hard to describe the impact that eagle had on our people: soaring to such great heights, its hunting ability, its vision. It was perfect for how we wanted people to see us.

Over the years we used lions, tigers, and bears. We brought in a shark, an orangutan (the one that starred with Clint Eastwood in the movie *Any Which Way but Loose*), and of course Sundance the eagle. To this day, MSA people still can recount stories of the animals, the messages they carried, and the themes they symbolized. The sense of anticipation for kickoffs was tremendous, because we never revealed ahead of time what the animal would be. And the message stayed with people; it lived because the messenger did.

ANIMALS NEVER STICK TO THE SCRIPT

We would choreograph most MSA meetings with some precision. But with the animals, we learned to leave room for the unexpected, something they specialize in. We (usually) took the precautions of using the best animal handlers. That was good enough for 90 percent of the animals' spontaneity. It was that last 10 percent that gave us a workout.

If you decide to go for the power of an exotic, living symbol—and it can be powerful—do it with a sense of humor.

One time, Ken Millen and I were going to a dinner at a Canadian lodge. We had a baby tiger with us that we'd had out on the road for remote offices to see (you want to include everyone in your campaign). That night, we were doing the animal handling ourselves.

When we got it out of the van we were in, the tiger broke away from us. It ran into the lodge and, following its nose, headed straight for the kitchen. We were chasing it like Keystone Kops.

The people in the lodge and the kitchen didn't expect to see an animal there, and they just went crazy. It was like the kitchen scene in *Jurassic Park*.

Eventually, we corralled the tiger and, with great effort and embarrassment, took him back out to the van. As we were trying to load him back in, he broke loose and got away again, disappearing into the snowy night. Off we went, calling, "Here, tiger! Here, boy!"

We found him later, no harm done. It was, however, the last time we took our tiger show to Canada.

The calls of Mother Nature were the most persistent problems with animals. Sometimes it happens in the middle of a performance, stage center. That's when you have to deviate from the script. In fact, I give full credit to animals for teaching me the art of ad-libbing.

We once had a tiger on stage that decided to let go right in the middle of my assessment of our competition for the coming year. Without missing a beat, I said, "That's what he thinks of McCormack & Dodge." The crowd roared.

Sometimes the problem isn't the animals' behavior. Sometimes just being an animal is enough. Once we had twin bear cubs that we'd been taking around the country to sales offices and user meetings. When we landed at Winston-Salem, North Carolina, our plane was surrounded by the police. It looked like a drug bust.

Someone had alerted the North Carolina game commissioner that we were bringing in black bears, which were illegal in the state. To make matters worse, the trainer was not a man of diplomacy. They arrested him and took all of us, including the bears, down to the courthouse. He was taken before a judge, where he indignantly showed her his documentation.

"These are my papers!" he said. "I've got permission!"

"Not in North Carolina, you don't," the judge replied testily. She ordered the trainer—and the bears—to be put in jail.

That night, I went before our meeting of salespeople and said, "This is the year of the bear!" I told them what had happened and how the poor creatures had been unfairly railroaded. I was just trying to have a little fun inasmuch as my main props were in the slammer.

Pretty soon, though, everyone was feeling pretty good. They began chanting, "Free the bears!" There was talk of "springing them." What had I done here?

Fortunately, no one resorted to vigilantism that night. The next day, we paid a fine and got our colleagues—along with the trainer—out of jail.

For all of the fun and excitement (and surprises) that animals can generate, the only real fear is of someone getting hurt. The fact that we used so many exotic animals such as lions, tigers, and bears always carried some risk. Cubs never were vicious, but they were strong and capricious. Full-sized animals always had trainers with them. We went fifteen years and never had an incident.

But in 1991, I was the master of ceremonies for a roast at ADAPSO. I'd brought along the largest cat we'd ever worked with, an eleven-hundred-pound Bengal tiger. At one point, while the trainer was walking it through the parking lot, a woman decided she wanted to pet it.

The tiger began to nuzzle her ankle, then playfully reached a paw around it and put its mouth on her leg. She panicked and tried to wrench away, and the tiger bit down on her ankle. Everyone jumped on the tiger and it let her go, but it had crushed part of her ankle.

Something like that certainly is distressing, but in looking back I wouldn't have changed MSA's relationship with exotic animals. Most of the risks were controllable (the woman shouldn't have been allowed to get so near the tiger), and the benefits were incalculable.

Certainly the animals were part of the showmanship that we'd incorporated into the culture. But they were more, too. They gave us drama, surprise, and humor. They gave us memorable metaphors. They gave us an identity radically different from anyone else on the scene. They inspired us and entertained us.

In the end, it didn't matter that they never followed the script, because life never follows the script, either. In a way, their spontaneity was a good lesson for us. It showed that we could deviate from the script and stir things up; or that we could respond to someone else's deviation and ad-lib our way to success anyhow. It was quite a ride. Lions, tigers, and bears.

Oh, my.

JUNGLE RULE SUMMARY

TO CONVEY A MESSAGE THAT LIVES, GET A SYMBOL THAT LIVES.

No one forgets the message or the messenger.

ANIMALS NEVER STICK TO THE SCRIPT

Don't forget your leash and pooper-scooper.

Part III

Keep your big company small.
                    —MSA adage

16

Jungle Rule #16:
When you mark new territory, walk toward
your horizons.

Change is a strange thing in business. It can be both exhilarating and frightening, and for good reason. It implies you're going somewhere you haven't been, but you're never exactly sure where that is. Change affects money, jobs, products, goals, institutional security, corporate and personal reputations, and prospects for future success. How should you deal with change?

Attack it.

Half of your opportunities in business will come by changing—intelligently—before your competitors do. If you fear change, the jungle will devour you. It's not a matter of striving for stability. The opposite of change isn't stability but stagnation. You have to change just to stay stable; you have to change aggressively to grow. Evolution is a process, not an event.

Ten years after the MSA phoenix had risen from the ashes of bankruptcy, it was clear that scarcely a day had gone by in which the company hadn't changed. The revenue had gone from $2 million to $73.1 million. We'd seen profits increase from $221,000 to

$5.5 million. Our employee roster had risen from fifty-seven to 1002. We had gone from selling two software products to selling more than three dozen. We'd established offices all over the world. MSA had become the largest independent application software company in history. It's time to relax and celebrate, right?

Nope, it's time to change. Again.

Even with what MSA's tigers had achieved, it paled next to what they believed they could do next. Theirs was an optimism born of their imagination, fueled by their success, and tempered by their tenacity. The problem for us was that the '80s, which were just underway, weren't going to be just like the '70s, during which Jungle Rules and tigers had taken us so far. The question became not *Should we change?* but *How should we change?* And what were the new rules to be?

Would there be an industry shakeout? Would mergermania overrun us? Would IBM and the other computer makers shut down opportunities to software companies as they built their own software lines? Would large mainframe computers become dinosaurs as personal computers took over? What about those Japanese software "factories"? Once any company begins asking questions about the future—regardless of industry—fear of change has to be replaced by fear of *not* changing.

Enter vision. How companies encourage vision—even *whether* they encourage it—has everything to do with how they manage change. Vision is the difference between adapting and leading. You adapt when you see where others have led; you lead when you see where others will go. Confuse them at your peril.

A company that continually adapts is inherently one without vision—or at least without the belief that it can realize its vision. Vision lets you lead change rather than adapt to it. That leadership is what will propel your company through the jungle, leaving predators to nip at the heels of the adapters.

So whose job is it? We've all worked in companies where vision was appropriated by the boss. No matter what anyone else had to say, they were wrong if they disagreed with the corner office.

Call it Castro's Law: *I'm Fidel and you're not.* Dictatorship is their prerogative, but it's a bad way to run a company. Or a country.

We came to have a different perspective at MSA. It was this simple: *Everyone has vision.* You've just got to figure out how to light the fire in them. If they have been actively setting goals for themselves—a requirement for business tigers—then they've gotten some vision experience. They just have to learn how to expand their field of vision from themselves (or their product or their department) to the company as a whole.

The job of the CEO isn't to put on a flowing robe and sit on a mountaintop waiting to receive enlightenment. It's to assimilate the views of the people around him and distill them into that thing called a vision. Ultimately, the CEO has to direct the future of the company. He can't shirk that responsibility. But the acquisition of that vision is a process that should involve everyone.

At MSA, we gave people a framework in which to find their visions. Then we gave them a process by which to share them.

Foresight begins with hindsight. The first thing we asked was that our people know what had happened in the last five years. They had to know not just what parochial things had affected them, but what broader changes had taken place in the industry. And now that we had become an international company, they had to understand the global picture.

Then they were asked to take that knowledge and project ahead five years—which should be the focal point for your vision. How do customers say our product line should change? Will we sell more to the same customers, or new products to a new customer base? What does the evolution in technology tell you we should do? What intelligence have you picked up on the street about competitors' plans? What do we have to do to maintain our position of leadership? What will the face of customer service look like in five years?

Bill Graves and I then had departmental meetings and companywide meetings. We articulated the vision as we had perceived it. Then we asked our people to question it, to challenge it, to participate in its evolution. The CEO takes what he learns here and combines it with his own perceptions gathered through industry involvement (trade associations, industry conferences, market research, and so on).

What you end up with is a vision that every employee has taken part in formulating and that every employee can buy into. It is no longer the arcane product of the wizard in the tower. It is *ours*—the most important pronoun in vision making.

Once you have your vision—which, like goals, should be expressed in a simple sentence—then comes the payoff for the process you've just engaged in: the mission plan. You lay out your objectives to realize the mission; then you describe your goals to meet the objectives; and, finally, you define the tactics that will help you reach your goals.

It is all done with everyone's participation. Because everyone was involved in defining the mission plan, they have a much keener grasp of all of the subordinate steps. And they have an entrenched personal commitment to execute the plan.

The mission-defining process never ends. You do it all over again every year, always looking five years out. You have to be willing to refine the plan—to change—as your business and the marketplace evolve. Then you invest where you speculate; you put your money where your vision is. You take some risks. And you communicate your vision to customers, employees, and investors.

That was the process MSA used to reach the top of the software world. It would be the one we'd use to find the next generation of horizons. Call it vision democracy.

TURN YOUR TIGERS LOOSE IN PUBLIC

The first vision that we derived in the early '80s was of a public company. In the prior decade, software companies tended to be small entrepreneurial ventures founded by technicians instead of businesspersons. They would fill some niches based on the proprietor's expertise, but niche filling wasn't going to work in the new decade.

Our vision foresaw software companies becoming strategic partners with customers, not selling them isolated products. That was going to take money. And a public offering seemed like the answer.

There also were problems. I share the following with you to illustrate the questions that arise when you're eye to eye with evolution that borders on revolution.

Only one software company of about three thousand had gone public at that point in time. There had been some fear from the investment community that because software is an "intellectual property," your real assets go home every night in the elevator, thereby leaving you vulnerable to transient employees.

Actually, I agreed completely that our real assets were people; but I disagreed vehemently that that left us vulnerable. We just had too many bright people on the same page of the playbook to be hurt by any small number of defections. And, luckily, we rarely lost people, anyway.

Beyond that, we also foresaw a revolution. The personal computer industry wasn't a business for hobbyists anymore. In 1981, IBM introduced the IBM Personal Computer. Suddenly, the world we looked at five years down the road looked much different from the one we saw yesterday.

Our vision interviews confirmed time and again that the PC was going to have an enormous impact on business. Mainframe computers, long MSA's bread and butter, were going to lose ground. People who'd never considered using a computer before were going to be conscripted into the revolution. Small businesses that had bought only adding machines were going to replace them with processors. We were convinced that only a public company, with its infusion of investment capital, would maintain leadership.

The downside was that we might be wrong. PCs couldn't communicate with mainframe computers and couldn't handle mainframe workloads; maybe they never would. Should we invest in as yet so unproven a market? In any event, mainframes weren't going to vanish overnight. Should we even imply to customers that we were migrating to other machines?

Beyond the technology evolution, there were other questions. A public company has onerous reporting requirements and demands for quarterly profitability with less regard to the long term than we were used to. Could MSA's vision even focus in that environment and still give shareholders some reason to buy our stock?

Could the company's tigers—the gunslingers, the burners—make the leap to conventional, civilized selling? Would they have to? Would shareholders frown on MSA's high-ceiling commissions and often lavish reward system for employees? Would public ownership bleed the soul out of the company? Many of us remembered the old MSA, the one that had been taken to the brink of collapse by undirected growth. Were we repeating the past?

Would we be able to maintain the intimacy with customers that we'd developed over ten years? Would we be able, in this era of corporate giantism, to keep our big company small—something we'd always regarded as central to our success?

The point of recounting these questions is to illustrate that the opportunities to second-guess yourself are endless. They rise in direct proportion to the magnitude of the change you're looking at. If you want to second-guess yourself, that's exactly what you'll do. It's a built-in escape mechanism for the reticent.

How you face change in those times comes down to the cultural decisions you make, not the fears of the day. You either attack change or you leave it alone.

In the end, it was MSA's tigers who gave us the confidence to move ahead. Even while knowing we faced uncertainty, we also knew that we always had attacked change. That was MSA's culture, and it had taken us this far. We knew the stakes were higher than they'd ever been—that the potential for growth was astronomical, and the chance for failure was coldly real. But we had a vision, our goals, and a tactical plan. And we had the people. The most common element of everyone's vision had been to see MSA continuing as a leader. With all of the risks, going public was the only way to get there.

And the tigers? Could they survive in a public arena? Among their greatest assets, remember, were versatility, durability, imagination, and ego. We figured if any species could prevail, it would be them.

Taking a company public often is the entrepreneur's dream from the day of incorporation. It had been mine. From our first year out of bankruptcy, we had published annual reports using the glossy format and reporting requirements of public companies. We had wanted to lay the groundwork, to establish the professional image, to show potential investors that we had an eye on a public future.

We made sure that the new territory we were marking took us closer to our horizons, not away from them. Then we devised a mission plan that everyone was able to buy into because they had shared in the vision. Then we did what had become almost reflexive for us: We attacked change.

If your vision is there, your plan in place, your resources lined up, and your tigers pacing, the only thing left is to signal the attack.

And that's where the CEO comes in.

DON'T SHED ON WALL STREET

There's no way I could try to illuminate all of the inner workings of Wall Street, even if I knew them. But I do want to share a look at a cog or two, and offer a perspective about why anyone would move into this glass house on a street of stones.

One of the relationships I'd struck up at ADAPSO's trade association meetings was with Al Berkley, a principal with Alex. Brown & Sons, Inc., a Baltimore investment banking firm. Although only one other software company had gone public, we'd convinced Berkley in the '70s about some of the waves coming in the '80s. He then became the first investment banker to specialize in financial services to the software industry. (He had seen change coming, attacked it, and by leading his competitors has prospered mightily ever since. MSA headed a list of seventy-five software companies in a row to go public.)

At the time he was primarily handling mergers and acquisitions. But the software industry was enjoying new prominence in the business world. I'd approached *Business Week* magazine about an in-depth look at the industry. Its editors had responded with a cover story and a multifaceted analysis that sparked a lot of interest in the financial community. Berkley liked where the industry was headed and agreed to make MSA the second publicly traded software enterprise.

One of the commitments I made was to keep my focus on the priorities of *business*. Sometimes if you believe you've joined the "big boys," your mind wanders off the ideas that got you where you are and to others that haven't anything to do with where you're going.

Part of the problem are the distractions of Wall Street. When we were a private concern, I was able to devote the vast majority of my time to customers, employees, and the marketplace. After we went public, I found a whole new tier of people demanding the most intimate of relationships: Analysts.

In a nutshell, analysts want to know about, and weigh the meaning of, every speck of dust that might affect stock price. Then they want to tell the world the good news or the bad news. They want to be the first to do it. And they want to look good. Theirs is a black-and-white world. And they don't hesitate to make their call.

Case in point: Dan Dorfman, an analyst and syndicated columnist, was once taken to a schmoozy New York lunch by Jack Berdy, the president of a company called Online Software International. The lunch tab, including a thousand-dollar bottle of wine, came to more than $1,300. A couple of days later, Dorfman wrote in his column how much the bill was and how glad he was that he didn't have to pay it. "That distinction," he wrote, "belongs to the shareholders of Online Software International."

There is no brotherhood of silence with analysts.

Conversely, when MSA later was suffering through a period of stock-price depression, we described our new plans to analysts. One of them, Steve McClellan of Merrill Lynch, wrote a terrifically insightful piece and gave MSA a vital "buy recommendation." That started our road to recovery and got the stock price back up.

Fact: They are there, they have power, and they want to hear good news. Providing it can be a cumbersome process, even for someone who loves the cultivation of relationships. But if you allow it to, it can devour *all* of your time. It wore out quickly for me because it was the wrong place to expend my energy.

Bill Graves, as MSA's president, was much more at home interacting with the analysts. He and Betty Feezor, our vice president of investor relations, began handling them on a daily basis. I ended up speaking to them once a year to present MSA's vision. As a group, they became the only people whose telephone calls I routinely routed to Graves or, later, Bill Evans, our chief financial officer.

The brilliantly lucid reality of Wall Street is that the only thing that counts is the performance of revenues and profits. Thus the best place for the CEO to be is not schmoozing it up with analysts, but making things happen in the trenches. When you make the move to a public company, the first pitfall is losing your focus. The second one is losing your company.

Having said all of this, I'll also say that I really enjoy heading a public company. The fact that we made $15.6 million in the initial public offering helped position us to attack change instead of adapt to it behind someone else's leadership.

But, like all of business, it's a game, and it has its own rules. And they're simple. You make honest assessments to analysts of where you stand. You make the numbers you forecast. You do it every quarter. You keep your promises. Nothing else matters. Including $1,300 lunches.

Your relationships in this region of the jungle become a little complicated. It is critical that you have good relationships with the analysts. At the same time, you can't endlessly interact with them without losing your focus on the business problems you face.

As odd as it sounds, then, your best relationship with analysts might be one in which they see almost nothing of you—because you're out making the numbers, planning the markets, solidifying the customer base, assisting the salespeople with the problems.

Keeping the promise.

JUNGLE RULE SUMMARY

WHEN YOU MARK NEW TERRITORY, WALK TOWARD YOUR HORIZONS.

You cannot change if you have no vision.

TURN YOUR TIGERS LOOSE IN PUBLIC

They can make the transition to new rules with style.

DON'T SHED ON WALL STREET

Tell the truth, keep your promises, and delegate the schmoozing with analysts.

17

THE TIGERS AND THE PEACHTREE

Jungle Rule #17:
Don't lose your humility in the jungle.

This is the anatomy of a mistake. I share mine with you so perhaps you won't have to make yours. I begin with:

The deal.

In the several years after MSA went public, we enjoyed a good run of growth. Revenue rose past the quarter-billion-dollar mark and the company stayed among the industry leaders. Our employee roster now had surpassed three thousand. Things were good on a lot of fronts. But one of the most indelibly etched episodes during that time was a failure—our attempt to spring, claws extended and confidence soaring, into the personal computer (PC) software market. I guided us to a perfect one-point landing on our nose.

The problem, in retrospect, was simple: we'd misplaced our humility. We'd lost our respect for the awesome power and complexity of the business jungle. We'd had so much success that we thought we knew everything about the software industry; and we thought we were powerful enough to dictate the terms of a new segment of the industry.

Well, we didn't and we weren't.

After we received cash from the public offering, we were eager to act. As always, we wanted to strike fast and move into a position of dominance, much like the one we enjoyed in mainframe software. I asked Bill Goodhew, one of MSA's vice presidents, to begin a search for an acquisition we could develop.

In relatively short order, Goodhew came up with a small, three-year-old Atlanta-based company called Peachtree Software. It was presided over by a fellow named Ben Dyer, whom I'd known through Georgia Tech.

We bought Peachtree for $5 million, a considerable sum. MSA now had its entree into the PC market. Although we'd paid a premium for Peachtree, we knew that most of the PC software companies were massively underfunded and pretty unsophisticated in their marketing.

We expected this to work to our advantage. With the capital from the public offering, we had the money to make Peachtree one of the most visible PC software companies in the country. Beyond that, we had the MSA name. We had the resident expertise of Peachtree's sales and marketing personnel, along with MSA's veterans.

To this point in time, we hadn't yet made a mistake. The acquisition went smoothly. The strategy—attack quickly, pursue tirelessly—was (even in retrospect) correct. The products were wonderfully complementary to MSA's.

The last problem was Peachtree's employees.

When the extremely smart but laid-back Peachtree workers heard they were being acquired by the largest application software company in the world, it terrified them. This was a T-shirts and blue jeans bunch, sneakers on the desk, "Save the Whales" on the ballcaps. All they could envision was Attack of the Pinstripes.

After the acquisition was done, I had my first meeting with them. I walked on stage in exactly the outfit they feared—wingtips, starched collar, right out of the IBM formalwear catalog. I spoke for a few minutes about MSA's background and growth, and said how excited we were to be working with them to build Peachtree into a powerhouse. They nodded, mumbled, wary at best.

Then suddenly I ripped off my suit and white shirt to reveal a T-shirt with the MSA and Peachtree logos merged. They roared. Maybe I was okay after all.

In short order, the two companies began working in relative harmony.

Unfortunately, neither of them was in harmony with the marketplace—the jungle.

Ask IBM. Ask General Motors. Ask Pan American. Ask me. Ask any company that's been to the top and walked right off the edge. When you're no longer humble in the presence of the jungle— you soon will be.

DON'T BELIEVE THE MIRAGES

Flush with money and confidence, we set out to forge a business that didn't exist. A horrifying mistake, this brings us to:

The illusion.

For the prior ten years, MSA had sold expensive software products to large, well-heeled ($40 million and up in revenue) companies that paid a lot of cash—sometimes hundreds of thousands of dollars for intensive service. For Peachtree's market, we were looking at companies with revenue from $250,000 to $12 million—the low end. It was a market we thought we knew anyway. In truth, it was as alien as Mars.

But in 1981, there were no entrenched distribution channels to reach that end of the market with personal computer software. There was the mail-order business and a few products available in retail stores, but there were relatively few computer stores around. That meant there was little expertise, and even less brand loyalty, from the candidates to sell the Peachtree software. This flew in the face of our traditional mode of selling, which was dedicated, high-expertise, person-to-person, problem-solving sales.

In the first three and a half years, we spent about $10 million on marketing, advertising, and promotion of the Peachtree name. We were going for a saturation level that most competitors could not compete with.

Our biggest opposition would come from the "phenoms," isolated products that became software megastars. The most dramatic example was Lotus 1-2-3, from Lotus Development Corporation. The company shipped its first product on January 16, 1983. By year's end, it had sold $53 million. A year later, the revenue from 1-2-3 climbed to $157 million. That's a phenom.

But in the accounting software world for personal computers, our marketing campaign for Peachtree had paid off with the highest name recognition in the industry. We decided that the best way to follow on our earlier success at MSA was to do the same things for Peachtree—which was more or less direct selling.

We lined up equipment distributors as well as computer makers. Their sales forces then would "emphasize" Peachtree products in their selling. We opted to keep the price high—around one thousand dollars—for most of the modules, then sell to the "high end" of the low-end market.

At one point, we had more than sixty Peachtree offerings. By the end of 1983, revenue from Peachtree had climbed from $2 million to $20 million. Peachtree's staff, which was at forty when MSA acquired the company, had grown to 175.

The illusion was crystalizing.

Then the distributors suddenly began to get phenom fever. The logical, structured, orderly sales and distribution organization we'd set up worked for a nonphenom world. But the product superstars—which didn't exist when MSA bought Peachtree—threw a wrench in the machine. Now the distributors "emphasized" the easier-to-sell phenoms. The computer stores already were doing that.

Prices were declining rapidly in the personal computer software world. They were going from strategic expenditures—which we knew something about—to petty-cash outlays, which we didn't. Suddenly no one in the network was "emphasizing" Peachtree's products. In the PC world, the tigers usually aren't people, they're products.

While the company still had high name recognition and extremely sound products, it lacked a phenom and the leverage that came with it. Distributors were following the path of least resistance in selling, and Peachtree had no backup plan. By the end of 1983, Ben Dyer had left the company. Distributors were returning unsold products. Losses were beginning to mount.

While Peachtree revenue had grown in 1983 to $20 million, MSA had poured so much money into marketing and promotion that it was only a breakeven operation. By the end of 1984, the sales network had soured horribly, and sales for the year were down 38 percent to $13.5 million.

The illusion was shattered.

We had allowed ourselves to believe the mirages created by the first rush of success and our own lack of humility. Instead of taking a sober look at a new world, we had pushed with money and swagger into a world where tigers, as we knew them, had little to do with success.

The lesson was simple: If you live by the mirage, you'll die by the mirage.

IF NOTHING ELSE, SALVAGE YOUR HUMILITY

With terrific pressure coming from analysts and shareholders wanting quarterly profits, we had only one option left: bowing out. It wasn't that we couldn't eventually have figured out the formula for success. It was that we'd lost our window of opportunity, which in a public company is measured in three-month increments. In a nutshell, we'd failed to figure out pricing and distribution—and thus we didn't become what Microsoft became. Which leads me to:

The exit.

We brought in Bill Goodhew, the MSA vice president who had found and recommended Peachtree initially, to head up the company. Goodhew, an experienced entrepreneur—and a tiger with full papers—took over with purpose. With some other former MSA executives in tow, they tried to return a more relaxed management style to Peachtree. They cut expenses and did what they could to revitalize morale. But while they made progress, the damage had been done.

The new distribution channels for PC software—the ones we hadn't anticipated—were evolving, but we were out of time. Peachtree was sapping MSA's profitability. In September of 1984, just three years after we'd rushed in with such optimism, we bowed completely out of the PC software business.

We began negotiations with a company called Intelligent Systems. We began by asking for $20 million for Peachtree. That was too high, they said. Period.

We talked to other suitors over several months, but no one was taking. In May of 1985, with MSA fully humbled, Intelligent Systems came back and offered to buy the company for the value of its assets—about $1.1 million. We agreed. It was done.

I got everyone together and tried to put the best face on the situation that I could. I walked out on stage and told them that the PC market was one we hadn't understood; that we'd committed too much money to the wrong way to do business there; and that, while everyone had worked hard, we had had no choice. We'd tried our dead-level best, and it just hadn't worked. "I'll let Kenny Rogers tell you," I said, then had the music come up over the speakers:

"*. . . You got to know when to hold 'em, know when to fold 'em . . .*"

I've said before in this book that a fight to the last person has no winner. That's true. I've also said that I don't believe in regret, because it accomplishes nothing at all. The key to accomplishment is forward motion.

But while I don't lie around lamenting the events around Peachtree or the conditions that led to it, I can objectively say that I wish I'd kept it. Had we been a private company, without that pressure for quarterly earnings, I probably would have.

Today, after arranging for a buyout from Intelligent Systems, Goodhew is president of an independently owned Peachtree Software. He had made a bold move to cut the price of the software dramatically and return to a mail-order business. One collection of eight modules, called the Series 8, had sold for $5,000. Goodhew cut it to $199 in order to get in line with the marketing tactics of competitors. In a high-risk move he took out an ad in the *Wall Street Journal*—three-tenths of a page for $413,000—announcing the new pricing. That morning, the phones began ringing.

Before long, sales topped $1 million per month.

Eventually Goodhew got back the confidence of the distributors who'd abandoned Peachtree. The sales network was revitalized. Today, the company is solid and profitable.

As for MSA, the experience corrected our perspective about where the power lies in business. It is the jungle, the marketplace, that defines the playing field. Companies just work there.

A few years later, we began to move again into a new vision of the PC software world, one called client/server computing. We still were confident, still aggressive, but this time the swagger was replaced with caution and analysis. In the end, all we took from the Peachtree episode was our humility.

It was worth it.

JUNGLE RULE SUMMARY

DON'T LOSE YOUR HUMILITY IN THE JUNGLE.

The forces of the marketplace work for you when understood and against you when ignored.

DON'T BELIEVE THE MIRAGES

You cannot kid yourself into success.

IF NOTHING ELSE, SALVAGE YOUR HUMILITY

If you take only a new perspective from defeat, it will have been worthwhile.

18

PREDATORS AT THE DEN

Jungle Rule #18:
When you're eye to eye with certain death,
don't blink.

If you live in the jungle, one day you will be stalked. Absolutely.
Positively. No matter what level of success you've had, the primal
forces of business will one day dispatch someone to upset your
world. They might want you, your key people, your territory, or
even your entire company. They want to remove your destiny from
your hands and put it in theirs. And if you blink, they'll get what
they want.

So don't blink.

The reason is simple: Predators want a meal, not a battle. If
dinner bites back, they might just hunt elsewhere.

On June 9, 1988, the threat was at my door. I received a call
from Charles Wang, the formidable chairman of Computer Associates International, Inc., a Garden City, New York, software giant
that had been on a six-year acquisition binge. He told me he
thought it would make sense to "combine" our companies. I informed him that I had "absolutely no intention of selling MSA" to
him.

But the call raised the hackles on my neck. Even though Wang had couched the call as a friendly inquiry, he was not the type to leave meekly after a "No, thanks."

Personally, Charles Wang is a likeable fellow. Bright, articulate, and funny, he also has a lot of the characteristics of business tigers—above all, tenacity and focus. But in the six years of CA's acquisition campaign, it consumed and digested dozens of companies, including some large, entrenched ones whose stock price had dropped into buyout range.

The pattern was usually the same: CA would buy the companies, then dismiss most of the sales force, public relations staff, administration, and management. The company identity always vanished. CA usually would retain only technical and product support personnel. The company had two thousand loyal salespersons and an extremely strong culture, but it just decimated acquisitions.

MSA was a perfect target.

Our operating revenue the year before had hit $258 million. We had a massive worldwide customer base, $50 million in cash, and at least $100 million annually in maintenance revenue. On top of that, we had become vulnerable with our stock price. Starting with the Peachtree Software purchase, some of the acquisitions we made did not do well.

By 1986, our earnings had dropped, and we were taking writeoffs. Our stock price fell from $28/share to $5 share. By 1988, it had only marginally climbed back to $8/share. We were in the middle of a major technology transition at the time, but it would take months—perhaps longer—to realize any gain from the transition. Meanwhile, we were vulnerable.

Charles Wang:

I called and told John we were interested. He said, "Please, I'm not interested." I wrote him a letter. It was a letter to him saying we were entertaining the idea. We have never done an unfriendly acquisition, and that would have been.

In the textbook definition of "hostile takeover attempt," he was right. And as Jim Liang of Alex. Brown & Sons pointed out, Wang had no history of hostile takeovers. On the other hand, one way or another, he always seemed to get the company he was after.

The problem was that the letter he sent to me that day had mentioned a tender figure of $11.50 per share. A letter of inquiry presents no problems. But when you get a cash offer, that's serious. In part, the letter read:

> *Assuming support from the Board of Directors of MSA, we would like to proceed with a cash tender offer for all of the outstanding shares of capital stock of MSA at a price of $11.50 per share net to the shareholders. This represents a significant premium, approximately 40% over the closing price of MSA on June 8, 1988, or approximately 60% over the normalized trading range of MSA stock prior to our purchases in the open market [CA had quietly bought three percent, or about 500,000, of the outstanding shares], and we think it merits support by you and the MSA Board of Directors and that it is in the best interests of your shareholders.*

That just didn't sound like a man who listened when he just had been told, "No, we're not interested."

While it was, as Wang stated, a letter to me, he said in the letter that copies of it were being sent to each of the MSA directors. I spoke with him on the phone and said, "We've received your letter, and we are not interested. We do not want to sell. Please withdraw the letter." He said he understood where I was coming from, but that we needed to talk, needed a partnership, we were old friends—that sort of cajoling. We didn't speak again until the battle was done.

As I said, eventually the predator will be at your door. When it happens, don't take your eye off him for even an instant. And believe only what your brutally honest logic—and the evidence—tell you. If it looks, walks, and quacks like a duck, it probably is a duck. But if it has blood on its fangs and is salivating on your toes, it's probably not a duck.

I'd always had (and still have) a cordial relationship with Charles Wang, but I knew for a fact that he very much wanted to get MSA into his stable. I knew we were vulnerable, and I knew he was adroit at hauling in his targets. And I knew he hadn't gone away when I'd said "not interested." Therefore the question became: What *will* make him go away?

While you're figuring it out, don't blink.

THE SECRET OF COUNTERATTACK IS PEOPLE

While you're not blinking, the first thing you need to do is gather a group of equally unblinking tigers around you to share your stare. Nothing disrupts a showdown like an army.

Because I simply wasn't convinced this was a friendly inquiry from Computer Associates, I treated the event as if it were entirely hostile. But this was the first time MSA had been cornered this way, so it wasn't something we were used to dealing with. And MSA's board of directors had seen little of similar threats. I needed outside expertise—a SWAT team.

When everything is at stake—and it was—there is only one kind of person to seek: the best. I called Maurice "Ted" Maloof of Hicks, Maloof & Campbell, a prestigious Atlanta law firm. Maloof had been MSA's longtime lawyer. He looked at what had transpired and quickly concluded it was potentially serious. I stressed that I wanted to attack this vigorously and with the best people. He recommended that we contact a fellow named John F. Olson, a securities law specialist with the law firm of Gibson, Dunn & Crutcher.

When Olson arrived, I knew instantly that Maloof had picked the right guy. He had the self-confidence of someone who knew every nuance of law and tactics in his field. He began by asking me what my goal was:

"Do you want to sell this company?"

"Do you want to sell this company to this man?

"What will happen to the people of this company if this takes place?

"You have a responsibility to the shareholders."

In effect, he read me my rights. I told him there absolutely was more value to MSA than what CA was offering, and that I feared terribly for MSA's people if CA was successful in this.

He then told me not to answer the telephone. Shortly after that, CA called. Olson picked up the phone and said with resonant authority, "One, we do not want to sell the company. Two, any offer you've given is way too low. The value of the company is much, much higher." Then he listened while the guy on the other end tried to intimidate him. He broke in, "Mister, I wrote the *book* [which he had literally done]. Don't tell me what I have to do."

The game was afoot.

But it was an excruciatingly tense time. If the offer were made public, a whole new rash of pressures would ensue. The stock price would go up, the media would be calling everyone for insight, analysts would be writing position papers. It would get messy. CA's attorney called and told Ted Maloof that we should go public with the letter. Olson said no.

Ted Maloof:

CA's guy said we were the only lawyers in the world who would say MSA didn't have to go public with this; that we were giving bad legal advice. He said, "CA will not go away. John can't crawl into a bunker and have CA go away." He said they'd sent the letter because they'd been rebuffed in the past. "What will you do when your stock drops back to eight dollars? How will you possibly justify this to your shareholders?"

The pressure built quickly. Wang and his team began calling my personal assistant, Mary Ellen Zubay. "I had one guy call and he said, 'You go in there and tell them they are *not* honorable men!' " she told me. "I said, 'You can tell them. I'm not going to.' "

Other times, they left shrill messages on her voice mail. Fortunately for MSA, she was the last person in the world who was going to be intimidated by blustering men.

Meanwhile we were thinking: These were guys who weren't interested in unfriendly acquisitions?

Then suddenly the letter was made public, Wall Street jumped on it and the stock shot up to $13.50/share. Now the rules had changed. Before it had been a state of high alert. Now it was "Man the battlestations."

There would be new pressures on stockholders. The morale of MSA employees, all of whom knew Wang's history of decimating acquisitions, would plummet upon hearing that CA was the suitor. The media would debate the union. Instantly the complexity of the fight was multiplied a hundredfold.

Now it came down to people. Great moments always do. We pulled the SWAT team together for what would amount to two weeks of nonstop counterattacking. Besides Maloof, Olson, Zubay, and myself, we had the board of directors—Bill Graves, MSA's president; Cecil Conlee, president of The Conlee Company; Robert E. Hicks of Hicks, Maloof & Campbell; and Clarence W. "Clancy" Spangle, retired chairman of Memorex Corporation and of Honeywell. The inner group also had Sig Mosley and Betty Feezor of MSA; Steven Bottum, David J. Callard, and James L. Liang of Alex. Brown & Sons; and Mitri J. Najjar of Gibson, Dunn & Crutcher.

It was as formidable a team as we'd ever assembled for anything at MSA. In the book *Future Shock,* Alvin Toffler wrote about what he called an "ad hocracy," a way of running a business in which groups of specialized people would assemble to solve perhaps a single problem, then break up, maybe never to be reunited, and set off for another ad hoc group.

MSA was used to convening ad hoc groups of specialists for sales presentations, problem solving for customers, creative meetings, and special events. But they usually were made up of MSA's own tigers. Now we were forced to recruit from other jungles.

Would they be able to attack in the MSA style? Would the chemistry be there? Would they care as passionately as we did?

At the center of it all was John Olson. Physically not an intimidating guy, he had an aura about him. It was unconquerability, that old tiger word. "John," he told me, "if you don't want to sell the company, then we'll figure out how to keep it."

Then he added, "Don't blink."

CROUCH DEEPLY, EXTEND CLAWS, SPRING

With Computer Associates' endless calls for me to crawl out of the "bunker," we knew Charles Wang and his team would be looking hard for an opening to force MSA's hand. Our job, on the other hand, was to foreclose every opening until we could shut out CA entirely.

Our edge, in the end, turned out to be something I've stressed throughout this book: relationships.

The first lesson was that, if you look hard enough, tigers can be found on the outside. John Olson and the rest of the SWAT team provided evidence. Olson moved into our offices for the next two weeks, as did we all. He began taking every phone call, fielding every question, drawing the line instantly at every attempt to weaken our position.

Before the letter from Wang, MSA had scheduled a shareholders meeting to take place on June 27. Olson and Ted Maloof advised us to postpone the meeting for two weeks. It probably would have been a dicey affair anyway because of our recent earnings performance. Because CA had become a shareholder, Wang was well aware of our schedule and undoubtedly timed his letter to coincide with the meeting. We knew we needed some more time to make our case.

Instead, we had a special meeting of the MSA board of directors and the SWAT team on June 27. There the board formally rejected the CA offer. John Olson elaborated at length on "the duty of care and the duty of loyalty of directors to the Corporation and its shareholders." What we were doing in fending off CA *did* have great implications for the thousands of people who had invested their money and confidence in MSA. If we couldn't get the company back up, we'd have done them a terrible disservice. But we all sensed we could do much better for them.

We sent out a letter about the meeting to shareholders. We advised them the board had received and rejected an unsolicited proposal from Computer Associates, but that we wanted the shareholders to "consider the items scheduled for this meeting in light of this development . . ." Specifically, the items were nine proposals that had been discussed in three previous board meetings that year, some of which now bore grave importance.

In short, they were antitakeover measures: reelect the board; remove restrictions on stock repurchase with capital surplus; eliminate shareholder approval for stock options of directors, officers, and employees; and eliminate certain personal liabilities for the directors.

If the shareholders voted for us, CA would likely go away. If they voted against the measures, MSA would be swallowed up. It was that simple.

The vote was set for August 4.

For the next two weeks, the SWAT team dug in. Wang and I never spoke directly, but battled instead in the media. Olson told me not to talk about higher offers. "Don't sound like you're negotiating," he said. "They could turn all that around in the media and get the stockholders against you."

But most of the time we spent on the telephone, talking personally to shareholders—in particular, Bill Graves and Betty Feezor. We set up a telephone network where absolutely anyone who had any connection to the vote could be heard. We gave out home phone numbers. No one who was handling any specific area went anywhere without telling us. If someone went to another floor in the building, we wanted to know.

This was where all of that time we had invested in cultivating relationships could pay off. I knew that we weren't faceless, remote, isolated figures to the shareholders. These were people many of whose families we had come to know. We'd spent time individually with them, had always taken their calls when they were concerned, and had always listened to their views about where the company should go. Many had become friends.

"The bid is undervalued," we told them. "This company is worth more than that; and we're committed to making it worth more yet. Would you please vote with management on this issue?"

On August 4, after hundreds of telephone calls and personal meetings, day and night for two weeks, the shareholders' meeting came up. The vote on the antitakeover measures astonished even us.

We had won 88 percent.

When the vote was announced, I went before the shareholders and thanked them for their confidence. I told them it wouldn't be easy, but I promised that their vote of confidence would be rewarded. I wasn't sure exactly how I'd do it, but I knew it was one of the most important promises of my life.

When we got back to the office, there was a phone call. I was sitting across the desk from Mary Ellen when it came in on her line. It was from Tony Wang, the president of Computer Associates and the brother of Charles. He said: "Congratulations on your shareholders meeting. Tell John that we are withdrawing. A press release is going out right now." Then he hung up.

It was over.

There were five lessons. One, don't give up something important without a fight. Two, when you fight, do it with the best people. Three, listen to the advice and counsel of people who know more than you do. Four, it ain't over till it's over.

And five, people are the key. Again.

JUNGLE RULE SUMMARY

WHEN YOU'RE EYE TO EYE WITH CERTAIN DEATH, DON'T BLINK.

Predators usually want a meal, not a fight.

THE SECRET OF COUNTERATTACK IS PEOPLE

A jungle SWAT team takes the best people you can find.

CROUCH DEEPLY, EXTEND CLAWS, SPRING

Turn the tigers loose.

19

ANATOMY OF A COMEBACK

Jungle Rule #19:
If you want to feast again, get hungry again.

"The hardest thing about being a success," Irving Berlin once said, "is that you've got to keep on being a success." Anyone who's ever gone into business knows exactly what he's talking about. The jungle gives you a thousand enemies to wreck your success; all you've got is the nagging conceit to think that's not enough to stop you.

It's a great attitude. Keep it.

As it was for many businesses, the '80s was an extraordinary decade for MSA. The company entered them fueled by a vision and a way of doing business that had been rousingly successful. Early in the decade, MSA became the largest company of its kind in the world. We continued to grow, had some success, made our share of mistakes, and, by the middle of the '80s, had our greatest prosperity.

But in the next few years, the industry began changing explosively all around us. The computer and software industries always had been dynamic, but things had gotten crazy.

One editor told me he was receiving an average of 1,100 technology announcements *a week*. And, usually, the bigger you get, the less nimble you become, and the harder it gets to change direction on a dime and stay ahead of all of that development. Adroitness is one reason why you try to keep your big company small. And that was where we began to fail as the late '80s came around.

Our mistake: We had stopped being hungry—at least hungry in the way we had been in earlier days, when every challenge was a meal, and our appetites were insatiable. And we hadn't done *whatever it takes* to get hungry again.

To regain that hunger meant making some hard choices; choices that were imperfect but necessary. It meant recalling some of the Jungle Rules we'd operated by in the desperate days after bankruptcy—rules about stalking goals, attacking dirty work, and doing *whatever it takes* to right things.

It had to begin with me.

In my role as MSA's chairman, I had been out of the office about two hundred days a year. I was traveling a lot, making speeches around the world, working on behalf of our trade association on industry issues, closing sales whenever I was asked in. But now I had to come in from the field and change my role with the company.

Bill Graves, MSA's president, had had the role of chief operating officer, running day-to-day operations. Graves had been with MSA since it was incorporated in 1963. He had been instrumental in its development over the years, beginning with sales—he was one of the best salesmen I've met in my life—and going right through his term as president. He had led most of MSA's acquisitions, had cultivated the relationships with Wall Street, and was well regarded in the industry.

Graves and I did almost everything together. We hired, sold, traveled, formulated strategies. He was, as he used to say about others, a sterling silver person.

But leading up to Computer Associates' takeover attempt, there had been problems. When some of the acquisitions began to go sour, profitability began to decline. Management's financial controls in the company had gotten lax and ineffective. One of our technology development projects had been something called Screen Paint, which was supposed to keep MSA ahead of the competition. Instead, despite 250 technicians working on the project, it languished endlessly in development while competitors leapt past us with even newer technology. The massive investment we'd made was essentially worthless, but Graves wanted to hang on a little longer. The CA gambit brought everything to a head.

When the analysts began demanding answers, they could not get them. No matter what else you do with Wall Street, avoiding them is the second-worst thing next to lying outright. The two staples of their meal are *access* and *honesty*. When they have questions, and they have a lot of them, they need to know the answers immediately. When they lose access, they lose honesty by default. The result was that the Street jumped on us. CA's takeover attempt showed us—and everyone else—our vulnerability, so in that sense it was good. We needed a wake-up call, and the prospect of losing the company was just that. But no one was explaining what we were going to do about it.

The next question was: What sort of a tremor will it take to make as massive a change as we needed? We had to right the company's direction, reset its goals and tactics, revive its profitability, and make believers of doubters. Tweaking wasn't the answer.

I consulted with MSA's outside directors. The discussion came down to Bill Graves.

Clarence W. "Clancy" Spangle:

Bill was really the inside man making all of the operating decisions. The business was going down in profitability and revenue growth. The board just decided that John had to come in and take over the running of the company. So we made the decision to let Bill go. It wasn't a very happy occasion. Graves had been with the company since the beginning. But we saw the action that had to be taken, and we took it. A lot of people in that circumstance would have had a hard time doing it.

The actual dismissal was the most difficult meeting I'd ever had with someone. Graves and I had known one another for more than twenty years, had worked together for seventeen years, had been chairman and president together for nine years. While we were radically different types of personalities, most people believed that it was that contrast that had helped MSA succeed.

But MSA had to get hungry again if we ever wanted to feast again. And getting there was going to take changes of such magnitude that it would be difficult, we reasoned, for Graves to embrace them.

In the end, Graves remained on MSA's board. We thought he would be better able to regain a perspective that would help the company. And he was.

Now we were able to revisit another Jungle Rule—*Concentrate on the survivors*—to get MSA on track. The Graves episode was difficult and, for many employees and industry observers, shocking. But it set a framework for future changes: Nothing was sacred; and management was serious about change.

From Peachtree Road to Wall Street, we had the attention of the audience.

MAKE BELIEVERS

It's fair to say that one of the most important things managers do is make believers of people. They make employees believe in goals, visions, and themselves, make customers believe in companies and their people, make Wall Street believe in products, strategies, and management. Making believers was at the heart of this comeback.

One by one, group by group, region by region, you sit them down and exorcize doubt. But there was so much to be done that it was hard to know where to begin. Between the time of Computer Associates' takeover attempt and the dismissal of Bill Graves, we had sought investors in the company. We needed to set the company up with both industry strength and investment dollars in a way that would keep predators from thinking they could move in. Something out of the ordinary was needed.

I'd invited IBM in to look at the company as a minority invest-ment. This would be an unprecedented move for the huge computer maker. While IBM had hundreds of working relationships with soft-ware companies, it never had actually bought publicly traded stock in any of them. If we were going to begin making believers of peo-ple, this was the dramatic start we needed.

But after looking over the operation, IBM came back and de-clined on the grounds that current management wasn't taking the company in the right direction. It was then that I made the decision to come in from the field and the board decided to act on the Bill Graves situation. Not long afterward, we asked IBM and other in-vestors back for a new view of things.

They wanted a little time to see how the company performed.

Meanwhile, I had to try to make believers of the most ten-ured pessimists, the Wall Street analysts. They already were squeamish about MSA because revenue had stopped growing at around $250 million, and the company had lost money for two years. Like IBM, Wall Street wasn't convinced that we could move the company ahead with the Screen Paint technology and a focus on mainframes.

At that point, we decided to write off the Screen Paint effort. It shakes a businessperson to his soul to admit that millions of dollars have been utterly wasted, but as soon as you know it, you have to act. The executive committee sat down with technicians, analysts, and industry experts and came up with a new vision. It would be a technology that allowed us to make personal comput-ers and mainframes operate in harmony. It would be called BrightView.

With the new technological direction in place, the management team reorganized, and the Screen Paint program history, we started the second round of making believers. It began with the analysts. But this time there was no schmoozing.

Steve McClellan, Merrill Lynch:

Wining and dining is no substitute for performance and delivering on your promises. After the stock crashed and the company had major earnings disappointments and Wall Street was very disenchanted, angry, and even disbelieving, John gave me access to come to Atlanta. This was right after Graves had departed, so there was a lot of shock and uncertainty.

I sat down and had lunch in his office. Simple little sandwiches. He basically laid out a strategy of what he was going to do over the next twelve months to turn around the company. In the past, the company had had dinners and wine for analysts at the local country club. But this was simple sandwiches and pretty much straight talk.

I came away from that meeting believing. I gave my positive purchase recommendation on the stock; sort of cast my lot with Imlay by believing he could do what he said he could do. Sure enough, within twelve months, things had begun to turn around.

It was an interesting vote of confidence to gather in. McClellan had a few years earlier written a book, *The Coming Computer Industry Shakeout,* in which he predicted that a lot of companies would do just what MSA had done, which was to get lost, and vulnerable, in the jungle. It was one of the most heartening endorsements we ever received when his purchase recommendation was published.

Next, we had to shore up the company's ownership. In early 1989, we struck up a relationship with a venture capital firm called General Atlantic Partners, which was then a little-known New York company that specialized in identifying undervalued technology stocks. One of the principals, Steve Denning, also liked the new direction we were taking. Like Steve McClellan, Denning was someone who would sit, listen, ask questions, observe, and cast his vote for the *people* he had confidence in. In March, General Atlantic bought 9.9 percent of MSA's stock.

But General Atlantic was a low-profile, risk-taking kind of firm. I'd only learned of it four months earlier. It was one arm of a business empire headed by a tycoon named Charles Feeney, who had built his fortune through Pacific Rim duty-free stores. Having the company in our corner was tremendous, as it turned out, but the process of making believers needed an even more definitive vote.

It needed IBM.

In May, we invited IBM back for another assessment of MSA. By this point, we had convinced a lot of believers, and we had improved earnings. This time, IBM said the direction was right, the management was right, the technology was right. For the first time ever it bought stock—in this case 5 percent—in a publicly traded software company.

It was less than a year since Computer Associates' takeover attempt, which effectively had been the Black Plague for whatever believers we had. Now we had new technology, new investors, a vote of confidence from Wall Street, and the biggest beast in the jungle in our corner.

When you're looking at a crisis of any kind, the second thing you do—right after you determine your new vision—is make believers of the people who can most influence the outcome. When they believe you're hungry again, they get hungry, too.

THE HUNGRY-TIGER DIET

Throughout MSA's entire life, the energy level of its people had been an asset. When the tigers were hungry, they prowled endlessly, stalked tenaciously, ate intelligently, and the company prospered. But when we reached the quarter-billion-dollar mark—when we had the luxury of enormous cash flow and millions of investment dollars—we'd let our hunger wane. We'd allowed some complacency to set in. We replaced hunger, and the dedication to minding the dollars and tactical follow-through that came with it, with a kind of automatic, three-meals-a-day suburban dining.

Our controls had become loose, our sense of focus had become blurred, and we had stopped rigorously challenging each other's ideas. We'd gone from lean tigers to fat cats, and now the company's future suddenly was on the line. We didn't want to trade our energy for timidity, but we had to rechannel it in more productive ways.

Enter Bill Evans. Just as John Olson had been brought in as an antitakeover specialist, Bill Evans was an anticomplacency specialist. In December of 1988, I asked him to come aboard as executive vice president and chief financial officer. He told me later that his first reaction was: "Why the hell would I want to join a company that's had as much disruption in the last two years as MSA?"

I portrayed it as a "challenge," which it was, and Evans responded. MSA needed someone to put some discipline back into the still-entrepreneurial thinking that characterized MSA. We still wanted to stay ahead of change, to lead by anticipation, and that required the entrepreneurial willingness to strike out in new directions. But we needed to get rid of the idea-a-day fast food we'd been subsisting on and devote our energies to fewer, meatier projects. The tigers needed a new diet.

Bill Evans:

The organization needed to be stabilized. We needed greater financial discipline, and better organization of priorities and tasks, roles and objectives. I think MSA's tendency was to jump from subject to subject—let's do this, let's get into this market, let's start this project. But there was a shortage of follow-through.

What I brought to the table was financial discipline. I questioned and challenged everything. I proposed ways to reduce costs and improve profitability. And I provided methodology to the management process.

MSA always had a lot of belief in its people and its

217

*energy. They always believed they could pull a rabbit out
of the hat.*

I didn't believe anything until I could see it.

Evans was a walking commercial for yellow legal pads. He took copious notes during even the most mundane meetings. And somehow it was all organized into a meaningful understanding of MSA's inner workings. Just as Gene Kelly and I had been able to go into companies as crisis managers two decades earlier and with fresh eyes see problems that had eluded management, Evans came in and saw through the haze.

If you came to a meeting with Evans armed with today's great idea, you learned quickly that wasn't enough. You needed detailed business plans, nailed down costs, market opportunity analyses, and the leanest plan possible for execution. It was utterly impossible to tackle any project complacently. Only passion would get an idea past him.

We had been able to make the tigers hungry again. Evans now made certain they ate right.

The results were dramatic. After two years and $100 million in red ink, MSA showed a profit after the first quarter in 1989. The profit increased again in the second quarter, then again in the third. The earnings performance was a catalyst in landing General Atlantic Partners and IBM as minority investors. Without it, we would have been just another company that talked about turnaround without really making it happen. Evans's financial controls—his diet—were utterly pivotal in MSA's comeback.

If you choose to embrace change as a management strategy, you have to do it intelligently and with discipline. While we always were proud of MSA's penchant for creativity and ideas, it is a freedom that can turn on you if you're not careful. There is a fine line between encouraging disciplined ideas and discouraging ideas altogether. Too much resistance in the creative process destroys the will to create. Too little resistance destroys the chances for success.

When you find the persons who can walk the line—as Bill Evans did—let them design your menu. Then eat all you want.

WAKE THE SLEEPING TIGERS

And finally—the sales force.

In just months, we'd made significant changes in management, shifted technological direction, begun rebuilding our bridges to Wall Street, attracted some elite investors, and put discipline and rigor into the financial controls of the company. That left the sales force.

No matter what else, if you can't turn them around, you lose. And they were down.

They had felt pretty beaten up after the Computer Associates takeover attempt. Competitors were challenging MSA's viability to prospects, saying we were technologically outdated and vulnerable to another takeover attempt. "Who knows if they'll even be around next year?" they would ask. The relentlessness in sales we were known for began to sound more and more like desperation.

But if there was one group whose mentality I knew, it was the sellers. When things get down—especially if the downcycle is protracted—sellers can begin to doubt, even when they've spent a career feeling unconquerable. And doubt always comes through to prospects and customers. What it takes to get rid of that doubt is a vote of confidence—and a win.

You need to gather them, rally them, talk honestly to them, and remind them that the company wouldn't exist without them. Not in a cheap, superficial, rah-rah kind of way, but from the heart. I knew what their potential was. These were the tigers who "brung us to the dance," as they say. I just told them we were still going to be dancing with them when the sun came up.

In January of '89, we hosted the annual sales kickoff dinner. It was probably the most important one we'd ever had. I absolutely believed that we had everything in place. If we could just revive their old hunger . . .

Brad Childress, former vice president, product marketing:

> *The sales meeting that we had in January of 1989 was the best sales meeting we ever had—and that was coming off a very bad year. We were battered and bruised.*
>
> *The theme for '89 was "Turnaround." The symbol was this little arrow that wound around in a loop and pointed up. Everyone thought it looked like the Jiffy Lube logo.*
>
> *We'd always had boisterous, raucous sales meetings, but this was the most spirited ever. We felt we could do anything after that meeting. John and the other managers had been able to impart such an empathy for the difficulties of the previous year, and such confidence in the launching of BrightView. We now had a product strategy that could keep us in the ballgame. But they said they were relying on a superior sales force. We left there thinking we could regain dominance.*

Good meetings can get the juices flowing, but winning sales is what counts in the seller's heart. One deal in particular we were working on was for a huge piece of business with Kloster Cruise Lines in Miami. Like a lot of sales, this one had come down to MSA and McCormack & Dodge. And it took on new importance.

M & D was ripping us every chance it had, trying to cast doubt on our ability to rebound from the problems, denigrating our technology. It was something they'd gotten good at in the prior several months. They'd won a number of sales from MSA just on the strength of the fears they could impart.

The Kloster deal had all the makings of another disappointment to start off the new year. Somehow we had to win it, even though in reality it was just one of many similar deals we had in the fire. Brad Childress was working on it along with Rick Page, the regional manager, and the area salesman. It was back and forth, back and forth. We knew McCormack & Dodge was filling Kloster's head with doubt, but we also knew that they still were McCormack

& Dodge—which meant vulnerable when it came to relationships with clients.

Brad Childress:

Once I told the salesman the deal just didn't feel right to me, that we'd better get down there. He said, "But they won't let us come down."

So I said, "Let's get on a plane and fly down to Miami, then call them from the plane and tell them we're on our way." We were in the air, so they couldn't say no.

We got there and found out that something indeed had gone wrong. If we'd just let things run their course, we'd have lost the deal.

A deadline had been set up by Kloster for making a decision. As we got near it, I joined the selling effort and had a chance to meet with—and, as it turned out, bond with—the company's senior management. M & D, meanwhile, had chosen to calmly await the decision from back in Massachusetts.

On the last day, we just camped out. We weren't going to learn anything until the decision was made, but our *presence* was, we thought, making a quiet argument on our behalf.

Finally Kloster came back with the verdict: The deal would go to MSA. We were jubilant.

In the end, they swung our way—past the doubts and fears M & D had tried to plant—because we had been so conspicuously committed to *being* there. Flying in when we "sensed" a problem. Answering every question from top management. Camping out in the final hours. In these actions, they saw a relationship. It was as heady a win, and for exactly the right reasons, as we'd ever had.

More important, it awakened the tigers. It was the kind of win that says: *It doesn't matter what anyone says about us, we're back.* Often that's all the message a tiger needs.

JUNGLE RULE SUMMARY

IF YOU WANT TO FEAST AGAIN, GET HUNGRY AGAIN.

Growth after success requires the same hunger as growth leading to success.

MAKE BELIEVERS

Once you have your comeback vision, make others believe in it who can affect the outcome.

THE HUNGRY-TIGER DIET

You have to encourage discipline in ideas, not just ideas.

WAKE THE SLEEPING TIGERS

The first and final tool of the comeback is sales.

20

THE COMPROMISES OF EVOLUTION

Jungle Rule #20:
Save the tigers.

In August of 1989, I was having lunch with Steve Denning of General Atlantic Partners, one of MSA's large minority investors. At one point, he leaned over to me and said, "I think we should explore selling the company to Dun & Bradstreet."

I looked at him with some surprise. Not because he shocked me by thinking it might be time to sell MSA, but because I'd recently been contacted by Dun & Bradstreet Corporation about just such a move. "I've got a meeting with Dun & Bradstreet in an hour," I told him. It was his turn to be surprised.

The evolution of any business takes stark turns. Often these turns are hard to foresee. My original goal twenty years earlier had been to own my own business in Atlanta. Then it was to have a major software services company "with a personal touch." Then it was to forge the largest independent application software company on earth. With the help of a family of tigers, we managed to achieve all of those goals—mistakes and roadblocks notwithstanding. But the eternal question in business always is: *What's next?*

At that point in time, two companies in the software industry were near a billion dollars in annual revenue and threatening dominance: Computer Associates, MSA's recent suitor; and Microsoft Corporation, the huge PC software enterprise that dominated the program market for small computers. The question for MSA became: How do we compete in that top tier of strategic providers? Do we even want to? Is it really so bad if we just handle our niche well and remain independent?

Every evolving business one day faces these questions. Your answers will go back to your goals and your people.

Even from the earliest days, MSA always had been a player, a force—as Brando would put it, a contender. When the industry was in its chaotic, entrepreneurial years, we had prospered by bringing professional marketing, management style, and customer service to the party. It had anchored us at or near the top for seventeen years.

Now the industry was changing—indeed, the world was changing in its use of information systems—and MSA had two choices: one, we could could stay independent, fund our own growth, and play follow the leader; or two, we could take the steps necessary to move back into leadership—with whatever compromises that entailed.

Option one was risky at best. With seventy-five hundred major customers worldwide, MSA remained an attractive target for a takeover if our stock dipped again. And the transition to the new generation of technology was going to be excruciatingly expensive—far beyond MSA's independent resources.

Option two had its own risks. If we were to sell MSA to a company culturally at odds with our own, it would be a disaster. The tigers who had taken MSA so far could rebel and desert in an oppressive, regimented environment where products were more important than people. By the same token, a company with the ability to assimilate MSA's people and provide them the resources for growth could find itself on top of the industry.

In the end, the decision came down to MSA's goals and people. As much as they—and I—cherished independence, it wasn't in their nature to play second or third fiddle. From the marketers to the technologists to the sellers in the field, they were contenders. And they deserved the chance to fight again for the crown. There was only one answer: Save the tigers.

It was a simple rule to state and a scary theme to grasp. But it acknowledged the evolutionary realities of playing the game in our industry. That acknowledgment is fundamental to any company not afraid of competing at the top.

Like customer service, you do whatever it takes.

True, the top is where the fighting is fiercest, the pockets are deepest, the ulcers are ubiquitous, and the falls are farthest. But it's also the tigers' playground. It is where everyone in business, either secretly or publicly, aspires to, but sometimes walks away from. We couldn't walk away.

The bumper sticker says, *"Life is full of trade-offs,"* and it is. So is business. There will always be compromises. The question is, which ones give your potential the greatest chance to flower? When you've made that choice, you've saved the tigers.

GETTING DUMBO TO FLY

The right deal at the right time. Simple, right?

If you get to the point in your business's life that selling it is an option, there are about a dozen reasons you might do it. They include: because you want out of the business, want to retire, want to be rich, don't want the responsibility, think optimum price is at hand, or because you've concluded the only way for the venture to continue growing is via merger or partnership with some other enterprise.

In all but the last instance, most people would take the money and run. But if your goal is to see the business on to better days, and you have some fidelity to your vision and your employees, things get more complicated. The most important consideration then is cultural. Does this proposed parent company have the management, style, attitudes, latitudes, temperament, money, and ideas to take what you've done and improve on it?

The problem we'd had with the Computer Associates takeover bid was more cultural than financial (although the financial aspect was important). MSA, a people organization, was at one extreme and CA, a pure product merchant, at the other; and the acquisition, had it succeeded, would have stopped MSA's goals—and tigers—dead in their tracks.

Fortunately, MSA was presented with another option. Dun & Bradstreet Corporation was a $5 billion New York City–based financial and credit industry powerhouse. It had been founded in 1841 and once had Abraham Lincoln on its payroll. Its president was Bob Weissman, a man I'd met at an ADAPSO meeting in Denver, Colorado, in 1970. At the time he was the head of NCSS, a software services company with great ideas.

Over the years, Weissman and I got to know one another, played a lot of golf together, rose side by side through ADAPSO posts, watched each other's companies, and developed a true friendship. After NCSS was acquired by Dun & Bradstreet, Weissman rose through the ranks quickly. In 1983, he led D & B strongly into the mainframe software business by acquiring McCormack & Dodge Corporation—MSA's archrival for almost a decade. Under Weissman's hand, McCormack & Dodge had gotten nearly as large as MSA.

In July of 1989, Weissman called me and proposed we discuss the possibility of D & B buying MSA. When we met, which was done in secret, the subject turned to the imperatives of advancing technology. The world was moving toward something called client/server computing.

In simple terms, it meant that computers would be splitting their workloads, from PCs to mid-sized machines to mainframes, and everything had to communicate with everything else. And it also meant reworking all of our existing applications software to utilize this technology. It was a development and reengineering effort that would cost hundreds of millions of dollars. McCormack & Dodge had to do it; so did MSA. "Why don't we join forces and do it together?" asked Weissman.

We knew it was the direction in which we had to go. Just as

important as D & B's resources and direction was its culture—strongly service oriented, high expectations, without a propensity to impede success by shoving unreasonable dictums down the throats of subsidiaries. It was a company that would let the tigers run.

Inside MSA, the code name for the negotiation that began was "Dumbo"—a word emphasizing the "D" and "B." Inside D & B, whose executives detested the name Dumbo, the code name was "Sheriff."

Still meeting in secret, Weissman and I began discussing terms of the acquisition. MSA's stock was around $12/share. Weissman brought in Peter Lessler, D & B's chief of mergers and acquisitions, who began by offering $13. I told him we needed $21. Sometimes days and weeks would go by before we received an answer. We knew there were executives at D & B challenging the deal. But we never forced anything. The negotiation game is one in which anxiety is your enemy.

The patience paid off. MSA's third-quarter earnings came out and were up considerably, adding leverage to our negotiating position. Lessler was an experienced negotiator, however, so he didn't panic. Finally I decided to draw Weissman back into the negotiations.

We met in meticulous secrecy at an ADAPSO meeting. If the press got hold of this negotiation, it would be horrendous. Every morning at 3:30 A.M., I would tiptoe out of my hotel room and meet with Weissman and Lessler from 4 A.M. to 7 A.M. in their room. We'd begun talking in July; now it was November. We all wanted to wrap this up.

Lessler was talking around the $15/share range, but while he was going in the right direction, we weren't there yet.

Lessler flew home from the ADAPSO meeting. On the train into work the next day, the electricity in his heart stopped. It was a freak physical phenomenon. He died instantly. I'd had Bill Evans, MSA's CFO, head off to talk some more with Lessler. "I called his secretary to tell him I was running late," remembers Evans. "She was in tears. Then she explained why she was crying. Suddenly being late wasn't so important anymore."

227

But Dumbo was in danger of crashing. Peter Lessler had been not only Weissman's colleague, but one of his close friends. The death was shattering for Weissman. We decided out of respect to Lessler and Weissman not to pursue anything for a few weeks. But we also knew that something—a press leak, cold feet, a new, hostile suitor—could screw things up and maybe take D & B out of the deal. Everyone held their breath. And their tongues.

Fortunately for MSA, Weissman himself picked up the negotiations when they resumed. He had been the champion of the acquisition when Lessler was negotiating; and Lessler had pursued the deal with his friend's enthusiasm. But we knew there were some doubters inside Dun & Bradstreet who didn't have Weissman's confidence. If they'd been put into a position of influence, they might have wanted to screw the price back down or demand other unacceptable terms. But Weissman had the confidence to keep the negotiation reasonable. We finally arrived at $18.50 a share. I took it to the MSA board. "Do it," they said.

On December 20, 1989, the tender offer was made to buy all the shares of MSA stock for $18.50/share—about $333 million.

The right deal at the right time. It's a simple concept that is defined by patience, tenacity, mutual goals, good faith, cultural cohesiveness—and the knowledge that, as good as the deal might be, it still is a compromise. If you can live with that, evolution is as easy as making an elephant fly.

SLEEPING WITH THE ENEMY

Imagine telling your children that you've just adopted the inbred neanderthal thugs down the street who'd been attacking them for years on the way to school. That fairly well characterizes the challenge I had in telling MSA employees about Dumbo. Not only were we moving in with Dun & Bradstreet, we were being merged with our hated, ancient enemy, McCormack & Dodge Corporation.

When you're faced with breaking news like this, the best way to do it is honestly, quickly, and with humor.

McCormack & Dodge was a company that we'd spent years motivating ourselves by denigrating. At one meeting, we worked MSA staffers into a frenzy by arranging for an orangutan to beat up on a punching bag marked with the M & D logo.

Now we were going to work side by side with them in a new enterprise called Dun & Bradstreet Software Services—or Oil & Water, Inc., as someone put it.

These are moments in which leaders really have a chance to lead. If you show fear, it goes through the organization like a bolt of lightning. If you show confidence—even humor—almost all of the fear can be eliminated, as long as you have a credible story to tell.

We began by gathering all of MSA's employees together. I spoke about the power of merging two huge companies, even ones who had been enemies, into an enterprise whose combined force would be greater than the sum of its parts. Then on a big screen, I showed news footage of German youths tearing down the Berlin Wall with pickaxes. "This is going to work," I told them. "Computer Associates is out and Dun & Bradstreet is in!"

Many were apprehensive, however, about being digested by a $5 billion megacorporation. When I introduced Bob Weissman, I used a video clip of him that he had made for a roast he hadn't been able to attend in person.

After speaking glowingly of this man I'd known for twenty years, I brought him out on stage. "This is our leader," I said. "Sometimes you fear big business, but you shouldn't with this man in control." Then I showed the video clip.

In it, Weissman is standing behind a podium delivering some hysterical barbs in his dry way. He is dressed in a tuxedo. You hear someone say, "Cut!" Weissman asks if the camera is off. Told it is, he steps from behind the podium to reveal he rented only a jacket and shirt. Standing there in these hideous boxer shorts, he says matter of factly, "No sense renting the whole tuxedo."

The audience loved it.

For Weissman, that simple willingness to laugh at himself in front of these people broke a lot of ice. In the audience, minds opened. We laughed. We laid out strategy. We came together.

Of course, the transition wasn't all that easy. The McCormack & Dodge people came with a lot of resentment. It was exacerbated when they learned that Frank Dodge, a cofounder of McCormack & Dodge and the chairman of the company, would become vice chairman reporting to me. In addition, the headquarters for the new enterprise would be in Atlanta, not Framingham, a decision they found incomprehensible.

Frank Dodge was devastated. He had not been informed of the negotiations by Weissman and felt snubbed. Weissman's choice to put me in charge and to put the headquarters in Atlanta privately grated on him. It was his worst nightmare. At the same time, he had been building this spectacular new office complex, from where he had planned to reign. It had three waterfalls, his own suite, and cost $80 million. You can imagine the shock to his system when he learned that corporate headquarters would be in a city that most of his employees still regarded as being without running water.

Dodge fought everything for a few weeks.

Then the Dun & Bradstreet management thought it would be helpful to get the two companies' top management groups together to get to know one another. The day after the deal was closed on January 5, 1990, we went to the Breakers Hotel in Palm Beach, Florida. It was horrible. It was like an encounter session designed by a psychologist gone mad. They had us playing games together—bonding, they said—including, of all things, hopscotch. I had a million problems to solve, and I was jumping into boxes. I wanted to address the people, but Dodge would have none of it.

The game playing solved nothing.

Finally, I had my chance to address the combined field operations of both companies together at a meeting in Miami. It was the first time these people, enemies for a decade and a half, had ever interacted off the competitive field. No horns, no tails. Everyone was human. I gave a speech with the theme "A Winning Combination," and talked about just how this merger was going to move both companies ahead. Fortunately, people listened. The healing had begun.

For all, that is, except Frank Dodge. He had a meeting with a group of his employees at the Dixville Notch. When I asked if I could go in order to keep after the unity theme, he told me I wasn't invited. I learned later it was a good-by party for him—he'd decided not to stay around as vice chairman—and that I had been the object of a lot of derision.

I wasn't bothered by his attitude toward me. It was pretty familiar after all those years. What did disturb me was his using company money to have a party whose purpose was to undermine what we were trying to do.

We ended up making concessions to our histories. We had wanted to keep MSA's lapel keys and the "People Are the Key" message for the new enterprise, but the M & D people, after years of loudly hating the symbol, couldn't swallow it. Finally, we adopted a new symbol and a new theme, all fresh and neutral, and brought everyone together under them.

Little by little, the venture began to show signs of the life everyone hoped it would have. The formalities that marked our communications began to ease into real human interaction. Some of it was just ice-breaking stuff that works well.

We had been sending out memoranda that were meticulously worded because they had been drafted by committee. The technical, formal sound of them prompted our British team to come up with a "decoded" interpretation of the phrases. They sent out their own memo explaining what we really meant. They wrote down phrasing they had seen in MergerSpeak on memoranda, then inserted "clarifications" in parentheses below it.

One day, out of nowhere, a memo appeared in our in-baskets:

"This approved concept"
(This idea has just hit us)

"is now essentially complete"
(was started yesterday)

"Results are encouraging"
(Hasn't bombed out yet)

"Return on investment is being quantified"
(We're still massaging the numbers so they'll agree with our answers)

"The risk is high but acceptable"
(With twelve times the budget and ten times the people, we have a 5 percent chance)

"This CONFIDENTIAL DRAFT is for your eyes only; it is NOT for discussion, comment, or critique"
(Make not fewer than fifty copies and distribute immediately)

The message: It's okay to laugh. Sometimes it takes someone with a little imagination—and protected by an ocean—to help regain perspective. In the end, we were just playing the game. Whatever we might have been in earlier lives, now we were together in the jungle and we needed one another to survive.

Sometimes that's what evolution does to you.

JUNGLE RULE SUMMARY

SAVE THE TIGERS.

However you evolve, keep the tiger den intact.

GETTING DUMBO TO FLY

Do whatever is necessary to control your evolution.

SLEEPING WITH THE ENEMY

Don't be afraid to think the unthinkable.

CONCLUSION: IT'S THE PEOPLE

There are twenty rules in this book, but there really is one message: It's the people.

It was always the people. When MSA was begun, it was because good people had a bright idea. When it began to decline, it was because people had lost their focus. When we needed to scramble so desperately to get MSA out of bankruptcy, it was people who came through. When we needed ideas, we got them from people. When we needed daring, we turned to people. When hard times hit, it was people who brought us back. It was always the people.

They are the sources of your triumphs as well as your failures. In management, in business—in the jungle—they represent the knowledge you do not have, the reach you don't possess, and the strength to make the difference. You cannot do better in running a business than spending the time to find good people, develop them, encourage them, reward them, make them believe in themselves, and help them realize their potential.

Throughout my career, I've been asked to define the business tiger. I hope this book does it. But the following description, one I've handed out to employees for fifteen years, succinctly characterizes the people I've known who were the key to success:

MEET THE TIGER

A Tiger is one who attacks a job with both zeal and impatience; who recognizes that productivity has dimensions of both quality and quantity; who despises shoddy performance and is intolerant of mediocrity.

Being a Tiger does not mean having a degree or taking prescribed courses or having a certain amount of professional experience, though it does embrace some of these elements. It is a way of life, a lifetime of study, a state of mind, and a relentless drive for excellence.

Being a Tiger means being extremely proficient in a specific field, interested in the job, willing to learn about it, study it, and grow with it. The Tiger is not only a specialist, but a generalist who understands an organization's overall objectives.

The Tiger may be hard to manage and will not be fazed by "that's the way we do things" or "that's the type of organization we are." The Tiger will ask "Why?" and expect to grow, but only through exceptional performance. The motivations of that person are objectives, goals, and accomplishments. A Tiger makes a great manager. A Tiger gets things done.

Congratulate the company that has several; pity the organization that has none. If you find a company with a full complement of Tigers, become a part of it. It is a priceless experience.

May top management have the wisdom to save the Tigers. They will certainly save us.

INDEX

Access, 212
Accounting department, 36–37
Acid tests, 77–78, 80
Acquisitions, 194–99
Adabas (software), 142–43
ADAPSO (Association of Data Processing
    Service Organizations), 86, 154–56,
    178, 189, 226, 227
  Foundation, 155
"Ad hocracy," 205
Ad-libbing, 177
Administration/personnel department, 109
Advertising, 43, 56, 82
Aiming high, 90
Akers, John, 88
Alexander the Great, 43–44, 45
Alex. Brown & Sons, Inc., 189, 202
Ally, finding, 10–11
American Bankers Association, 54–55, 130
  Automation Conference, 130
American Software, Inc., 29
"America's Best-Dressed Businessman"
    award, 153–54
Analysts, 190–92, 197, 212, 214
Anecdotes, 85–86
Animals, live, 3, 4, 46, 173–79

Annual bonus, 64
Anticomplacency specialist, 217
Apple Computer, 134
Application software, 25, 37
Aristotle, 43
"Athletes," 74
Atlanta Falcons, 138
Atlanta Journal, 57
Audience, capturing, 84–85, 131
Augusta Courier, 92
*Automated calling, 5
Automatic Data Processing, 156
Autonomy, 66, 129, 139
  and company environment, 15
  and control, 11, 12, 31–32
  excess, 17–18
  and giving permission not to seek your
    permission, 157–63, 163

Bankers, 37
Bank of New York, 66
Bankruptcy, 26, 33, 37, 41–42
  collections during, 62–64
  emergence from, 57, 66, 71–80
  and humor, 86
  and image, 53–55

Bankruptcy, *(cont.)*
  as selling point, 51–52, 100
  and *whatever it takes*, 60–67
"Bankruptcy Ain't So Bad" slide presentation, 46, 87
Barna, Becky, 151
Battel, Gen. William, 96–97, 98
Bears, live, 177–78
"Beer drinking" test, 77
Berdy, Jack, 190
Berkley, Al, 189–90
Berlin, Irving, 210
Big company, keeping small, 134–35
Board of directors, 18, 206, 207, 213
Boeing Computer Services, 57
Bottom-up selling, 90
Botts, Bill, 30–31
Bottum, Steven, 205
Boundaries, 159–61, 163
Brevity, 146, 149, 150
BrightView, 214
Brooks, Bonnie, 165
Bush, George, 138
Business plans, 218
Business theater, 3
Business Week, 134, 190
Butkus, Dick, 56
Byrd Press, 169

Callard, David J., 205
Calloway, Bo, 91
"Carpe diem" rule, 27
Cash shortages, 35, 60–64, 167
Cash tender offer, 202
Castro's Law, 185
Casualties, 35
Catchpole, Jackie, 141–42
Catchpole, Lawrence, 141, 142
Cavett, Dick, 83
Celebrities, 55–56, 98
Cellular phones, 43
Change, 19, 157, 183–92, 192, 218
Chapter X (National Bankruptcy Act), 37
Charles, Prince of England, 84
Childress, Brad, 220–21
Chrysler Corporation, 12
Chu, Twon, 144
Civilities, 3, 136
  as weapon, 125–26, 132
Clarity, 43
Cleveland Bank and Trust Company, 33
Client/server computing, 199
Closing deals, 64–66, 96–97, 100
Clubs for elite performers, 109
Coca-Cola, 57, 136
Code generator, 13
Code of conduct, 116
Collections, 62–64
College graduates, hiring, 76, 78
Comeback, 210–22
Coming Computer Industry Shakeout, The
  (McClellan), 215
Communication, 146–56

  and humor, 82, 83–84
Compensation, 106–20, 188
Competition (competitors), 2, 3, 49, 155, 219
  and imagination, 130–31
  importance of, 121–32
  outservicing, 166–68, 172
Competitiveness, 73, 75, 80
Competitor of the Month, 123, 124
Compromises, 225
Computer Associates International, Inc.
  (CA), 200–209, 211, 219, 224, 226
Computer centers (service bureaus), 16, 24, 31, 35
Computer Sciences Corporation (CSC), 41
Computer Technology/South (CT/South),
  19–20, 23, 24
Computing, and technicians vs.
  businesspersons, 53–54
Conferences, 82
Confidence, 66
Conlee, Cecil, 205
Consultants, 19, 24, 31
Contracts, 23, 24
Control
  and autonomy, 31–32
  and goals, 11–12, 14–15
  goals beyond, 15–17, 22,
  not losing 17–18,22, 28, 29
Conventions, 130–31
Corporate culture, 73, 81–82, 86, 162
  and selling company, 224, 225–28
Costs, 218
Counterattack, secret of, 203–206
Courage, 73, 80
Creativity, 1, 159, 163
  and evolving idea, 55
  and humor, 81, 84
  and tigers, 73
Creditors, 18, 26, 28, 39, 113
Crisis
  as best place to start, 19–21, 22
  and building tiger's den, 35–39
  and collections, 62–64, 67
  concentrating on survivors during,
  41–43, 58
  domino effect of, 17–18
  and honesty, 34–35
  turning, into selling points, 51–52, 58
Crisis managers (management), 18, 19–21,
  23–29
Criticism, overcoming hostile, 45–46
Customer Council, 168
Customer is king theme, 165
Customer of the Year, 165
Customers (customer relationships)
  angry, 49–50
  attempt to fire, 33–34
  and collections during bankruptcy,
  62–63
  conferences with, 55
  and confidence, 67
  and convention, 3

Customers, *(cont.)*
  as database files vs. people, 5
  getting into skin of, 170–72
  and goals, 14
  greeting, 12, 14
  and humor, 81
  and key symbol, 48
  as king of jungle, 164–73
  motivating prospects to become, 53–57
  tracking mindprints of, 169–70
Customer satisfaction
  and leading by example, 49–50
  and marketing, 48
Customer service, 166–68
  and selling, 101–103, 105
  and *whatever it takes*, 60, 64, 66

Danger, laughing in face of, 86–87
Darnell, Charlie, 168
Datamation Magazine, 151
Data processing managers, 25, 123
Deadlines, 64
"Death of the Mini" funeral, 152–53
Debt, 17, 18, 28
  for equity, 39
Decision-making
  as compensation, 109
  and control, 11–12
  and seizing the day, 27
Deere & Company, 137
Democracy of ideas, 11
Dennig, Steve, 215–16, 223
Department heads, 47
Detroit Tigers, 5
Developers, 99
Dirty work, 31–40, 211
Dishonesty, 116
Distribution, 196–97, 198, 199
Dodge, Frank, 230, 231
Doers, 78
"Doing the right thing," 141–43, 145
Doing what is necessary, 13. See also
      Whatever it takes
Dorfman, Dan, 190
Doubts, attacking, 44–46, 48, 58
Drucker, Peter, 56
Dun & Bradstreet Corporation, 2, 48
  MSA sold to, 223, 226–32
Dun & Bradstreet Software Service, Inc.,
      5–6, 98, 124, 141, 223, 229
Durability, 73, 80
Dyer, Ben, 197

Eagle symbol, 175–76
Earnings, 14
Eastwood, Clint, 176
Edenfield, Jim, 16, 17, 28–29
Edenfield, Judge Newell, 37, 38–39, 51,
      61, 63, 67, 168
Education, and hiring, 76, 78–79
Educational system, 5
Ego, and compensation, 109–10
Eisenhower, President Dwight D., 45

Electronic Data Systems, 12
Electronic mail, 5, 135
Eli Lily, Inc., 57
Elson, Ed, 171–72
Emery, Walter, 136
Emotion
  and motivation, 43
  and key symbol, 47–48
  and selling, 97
Empathy, 74, 80, 129
Employees
  compensation and rewards, 106–20
  and convention, 3
  firing, 30–33
  and humor, 81, 86
  motivating survivors, 43
  and personal recognition, 139
  and vision, 184–85
Energy, 72, 80
Entrepreneur, 3, 11, 75
Environment, company
  and compensation, 108–109, 111
  and goals, 15
  See also Corporate culture
Ethics, 59, 60. *See also* Code of conduct
Evans, Bill, 191, 217–18, 227–28
Evolution, 223–32
Example, leading by, 49–50, 58
Excess, 17, 19
Execution, 4, 41–58
Exploitative people, 116

Facilities management (FM), 19
Failure
  grand, of employees, 139–40
  and humility, 193
Fairness, 35
Family
  employees', 110
  of tigers, 99–101, 104
Fate, 10
"Fatty the Chairman," 84–86
Federal Reserve Banks, 64–65
Feeney, Charles, 216
Feezor, Betty, 191, 205, 207
Field sales, 11–12
Fight to last person has no winner, 30–40,
      198
Financial discipline, 217–18
Financials, 36–37
Financial Technology, Inc., 103–104
Fire, as tool, 46
Firing people, 23, 24, 30–35, 41, 42
  and motivating survivors, 44–45
First City National Bank of Houston, 130
First impressions, 14
First Nationsl Bank of Atlanta, 16–17, 24,
      31, 53, 137
Fisher, Jeff, 103
Fitts, Grant, 113–13
Flair, 151–54, 156
Football, 13
Ford, Gerald, 56, 100–101

Forgiveness, 129, 158, 159
Forrester, Jay, 106, 107, 111
Fort Benning, Georgia, 93–94
Fox. See *Semper fidelis*
Franklin, Benjamin, 140
Freedom to think on your feet, 14–15. *See also* Autonomy
Fresh eyes, 18, 19, 24, 218
Friendships, 136–37, 140–41, 145
  and media, 150–51
Future Shock (Toffler), 205

Gates, Bill, 78–79, 157–58
General Atlantic Partners, 215–16, 218, 223
General Motors, 195
Georgia, University of, 13
Georgia Institute of Technology (Georgia Tech), 15, 16, 30, 78
Gibson, Dunn & Crutcher, 203
Gifford, Frank, 56
Glover, Bill, 144
Goal(s)
  beyond your control, 15–17, 22
  helping customer reach, 57
  and knowing what you're fighting for, 39
  -mindedness, 74, 80
  and recognizing performance, 113
  setting, 10, 12–15, 21, 28–29
  and specifics, 9–10, 13
  stalking, 9–22
  stating new, to regain control, 17–18
Goal sharing, 10–12, 21
  with customer, 50, 164–72
  and listening, 97
  and marketing, 48
  and media, 149
  and sales, 52
  with sales people and employees, 108–9
  with survivors, 43
Gods Must Be Crazy, The (movie), 46
Golf, 98, 136–37
Gone With the Wind (movie), 46, 87
Goodhew, Bill, 194, 197–98, 199
"Go-to" bunch, 37
Grambling State University, 10–11
Graves, Bill, 15, 17, 33, 34, 47, 75, 77, 167–68, 185–86, 191, 205, 207, 211–13, 215
Grimes, George, 33
Growth, 16, 183–92, 193
Grudge, not holding, 128–29
Gulf Life Insurance, 113–14
Gunslingers label, 71, 116

Hall of Fame, 13
Heading off, 147
Healthcare systems company, 31
Helicopter rides, 131
Henderson, Russ, 16, 152–53, 173–74
Hicks, Robert E., 37, 38, 39, 62, 67, 205
Hicks, Maloof & Campbell, 203

Hiring, 75–80
Homework, 98
Honesty, 1
  and analysts, 212
  and crisis, 34–35, 40
  and media, 148–49
  and motivating people, 43
Honeywell, 16, 79, 91, 92, 111, 144, 152, 168, 173
Honeywell, Inc. v. Lithonia Lighting, Inc., 168
Hooks, 43, 46
  celebrities as, 56–57
  See also Animals, live
Hornung, Paul, 56
Hostile acquisition, 2, 200–209
House, Don, 25
Houston National Bank, 130
Howard, Harry, 45, 160
Human resources, 75
Humility, 193–99
Humor, 3, 177, 232
  as management tool, 81–89
  and motivating survivors, 46
  and public speaking, 83–86
  and sacred cows, 87–89
Hungry, staying, 211–22
Hungry-tiger diet, 216–19, 222

Iacocca, Lee, 12
IBM, 25, 34, 54, 79, 87–88, 91, 92, 94, 107, 134, 152–53, 155, 157–58, 168, 184, 187, 195, 214, 216, 218
Icons, as company soul, 46–47, 47
Ideas, nine lives of, 55–57, 58
Illusion, 195–97
Imagination, 4
  and company environment, 15
  and company image, 54
  and grand themes, 162
  as key marker of tiger, 73, 80
  and killer instinct, 130–31, 132
  to motivate survivors, 43
Imlay, Geri, 154
Imlay, Jerry, 35
Imlay, Scott, 144
Immutable Truths, 1
Indiana University, 13
Influence, 109
Information, 11, 12, 31, 139
Information Systems, 79
Initiative, 15
Insurance, 110, 142
Integrity, and hiring, 79–80
Intelligent Systems, 198–99
International Computer Programs, Inc. (ICP), 139
Interviewing, 75–77, 80
Intrapreneurship, 11

Japan, 150, 155, 184
Jensen, A. P. "Pete," 30, 34, 79
Jones, Robert Tyre, Jr. "Bobby," 125–26,

Jones, Robert Tyre, Jr. "Bobby," *(cont.)*
    136, 140
Judges, 37
Jungle
    clock, 64–65
    defined, 1–2, 4
    in high-tech world, 6
    interview, 75–77
    selling, 90–105
    selling, and boundaries, 160–61
Jungle Rules
    defined, 1, 3–4
    #1: *Believe in fate, but stalk your goal,*
        9–22
    #2: *Lay out your plan, then strike like a*
        cat, 23–29
    #3: *A fight to the last person has no*
        winner, 30–40
    #4: *Concentrate on the survivors,* 41–58,
        213
    #5: *Don't be afraid of* whatever it takes,
        59–67
    #6: *Never hunt for tigers just to put them*
        on a leash, 71–80
    #7: *Where the jungle is darkest, use humor*
        as the light, 81–89
    #8: *Sell it in the treetops,* 90–105
    #9: *If you capture dinner, you get to eat it,*
        106–20
    #10: *If a competitor is stalking you,*
        extinction will not, 121–32
    #11: *Build a front porch on your*
        treehouse, 133–45
    #12: *Tigers need only a scent to set them*
        on the hunt, 146–56
    #13: *Give your permission not to seek*
        your permission, 157–63
    #14: *The king of the jungle is the customer,*
        164–72
    #15: *To convey a message that lives, get a*
        symbol that lives, 173–79
    #16: *When you mark new territory, walk*
        toward your horizons, 183–92
    #17: *Don't lose your humility in the*
        jungle, 193–99
    #18: *When you're eye to eye with certain*
        death, don't blink, 200–209
    #19: *If you want to feast again, get hungry*
        again, 210–22
    #20: *Save the tigers,* 223–32

Kahn, A. D., 37, 67
Kelly, Gene, 2, 19–20, 24, 26, 27, 28, 31,
    32–33, 36, 44, 45, 62, 63, 64, 128,
    218
Kennedys, 92
Kerr-McGee, 57
Key symbol, 47–48
"Keybuster Awards," 48, 128
Kissinger, Henry, 53, 56
Kloster Cruise Lines, 220–21
Knight, Bob, 13, 24
Knowledgeware, 13–14

Lasorda, Tommy, 56, 131
Lautenberg, Frank, 156
Lawyers, 37
Leaders (leadership), 15
    and crisis, 21, 45–46
    by example, 49–50
Leasing contracts, 168
Legality, 59, 60
Lessler, Peter, 227–28
Liang, James L. "Jim," 202, 205
Lithonia Lighting, Inc., 168
Listening
    to competitor, 126–28, 132
    for ways to share goals, 97
"Little People's Day," 92
Losing, 73
Lotus 1-2-3, 196
Lowe, Twila, 14, 15, 175
Loyalty, 143–45

McCain, E. W. "Mac," 19, 96–97
McClellan, Steve, 191, 215
McCormack Dodge Corporation (M &
    D), 48, 124, 127–28, 151, 169,
    170, 177, 220–21, 226–27, 229,
    230–32
MacElhattan, Jerry, 33
MacIntyre, Doug, 122, 147, 169–70
McSpaden, Jud, 136–37
Maddox, Lester, 91–92
Magnolia tree, 165–66
Maguire, John, 142–43
Mailer, Norman, 109
Mainframes, 187
Maintenance fees, 167
Making believers, 213–16, 222
Making tracks, 154–56
Maloof, Maurice "Ted," 19–20, 37,
    203–204, 205, 206
Management (managers), 15, 18
    and Alexander the Great, 44
    tools, 3, 81–89
    See also Leaders
Management Science America, Inc. (MSA),
    6, 13, 14
    attempted takeover, 200–209
    and autonomy, 160–61
    bankruptcy, 37–38, 51–52, 113
    after bankruptcy, 81–89
    and communication, 151–53, 155, 156
    comeback of, 2, 19–20, 24, 25–26
    and compensation, 109–12
    and competition, 121–22, 124, 127–28,
        130–31
    Cup, 109
    and customers, 165–66, 167, 168
    firings, 30–34
    founding and crash of, 15–17
    goals, 28–29
    goes public, 175, 187–92
    growth, 183–84
    hiring, 75–80

Management Science America, Inc. (MSA), *(cont.)*
  and key symbol, 47–49
  leaders set example at, 49–50
  motivating survivors at, 44–45
  Peachtree acquisition, 194–99
  and personal relationships, 135–36, 143–44
  reversing image, 53–57
  Rookie of the Year Award, 14
  sales strategy, 91, 92–93
  sold to Dun & Bradstreet, 223–32
  and staying hungry, 210–22
  and stock ownership, 118–19, 120
  tiger's den at, 36–38
  and tiger symbol, 174–75
Marketing, 14, 16
  and humor, 81
  and people, 48
  product promotions, 56
  and symbols, 47
Markets and marketplace, 4, 43, 199
Marshal, Marty, 135
Martin, Billy, 128
Mattel company, 88
Matthews, Bill, 24, 31
Media, 148–51, 156
  and takeover attempt, 207
Merrill Lynch, Pierce, Fenner and Smith, 57
Merritt, Mervin, 2
Message, conveying, 173–79
Microsoft Corporation, 78–79, 134, 157–58, 224
Millen, Ken, 75–76, 175–76, 177
"Mindprints" of customers, 169, 172
Minicomputers, 152
Minnesota Vikings, 12, 13
Mirages, 195–97, 199
Morale, 18, 45
Morgan, Pete, 175
Mosley, Ivan Sigmund "Sig," 36, 205
Motivation
  of customers, 53–55
  people as key to, 43–44, 47–48
  of survivors, 44–46, 51
  tools for, 46
  See also Symbols

Najjar, Mitri J., 205
Namath, Joe, 50
National Computer Conference, 155–56
NCSS, 226
Networking, 156
Newberry, Dr. Tom, 15, 17, 28–29
New York Giants, 12, 13
"Nicing 'em to death," 125–26, 132
Notes, personal, 138–39
"Not-Invented-Here" syndrome, 123

Office romances, 117
Old or conventional rules, 15, 51
  vs. *whatever it takes*, 60

Olson, John F., 203, 205–207, 217
100 Percent Club, 113
Online Software International, 190
Opportunity, 27–29, 36, 183
Organization, 4
"Outsiders," 18
  and tiger's den, 37–39
Ownership
  as goal, 26–29
  as motivation, 118–19, 120

Packaging, 43
Page, Rick, 101, 102, 220
Paine, Webber, Jackson and Curtis, 57
Pan American, 195
Parking places, 110
Passions, 160
  and selling, 98
Payroll
  meeting, 60–61
  system problems, 66
Peachtree Software, 150–51, 194–99, 201
Peek, Burton, 137
Peer support, 109
Peller, Clara, 81
People
  follow examples, 49–50, 58
  as secret of counterattack, 203–206
  skills, 3, 5–6
  and success, 4
People are the key rule, 6, 58, 231
  and competition, 127
  and letting no one go unnoticed, 114–15, 120
  and motivating tigers, 43–44
  as MSA icon and message, 47
  and pricing, 104, 105
  as primary message, 233–34
  and revitalizing survivors, 45–50
  and spouses of employees, 110
  and swarmselling 101–102
Performance figures, posting, 113
Perks, 109–11
Perot, Ross, 12
Persistence, 1
Personal computers, 43, 135, 152, 187–88
  software, 193, 196–98
Personal interaction, 135, 145
Personal service, 48, 50
Personifying enemy, 122–24
Personnel problems, 18
Phippen, John, 88
Phoenix, 7
Plan
  laying out, 29
  and striking, 25–26
Playboy Enterprises, 57
"Position, in position to be in," 13, 14, 61–62
Predators, 200–209
Presentations, 87
Presidential Library, Gerald Ford, 100

President's Council, 109–10, 111, 113, 117
Pressure, 64–66, 67
Price
  cutting, 12
  negotiating, 64–65
  of PC software, 196–97, 199
  psychology of, 103–104, 105
Problem solving (solvers), 14, 15
  and customer service, 168
  and salesman, 15, 97, 158–59, 160–61
  and software, 56
Productivity, 6
Product(s), 4, 14, 43
  guardians, 37
  support, 60, 99, 103
Profitability, 159–61, 211–12
Programmers, 25
Programming Methods, Inc., 61
Project leadership, 11
Prominence, 109
Promises, 3, 64, 99, 191, 192
Promotions, for employees, 111
Prospects
  motivating, 43, 53–57
  and swarmselling, 102
Public, going, 186–92, 194
Publicity, 148–51
  and "secrets," 53–55
  See also Media

Quality control, 5
Quarterback, vs. winner, 15
Questions, and selling, 97
Quotability, 149
Quotas, 64

Receptionist, 14, 99
Recession, 17
Recognition, 109, 110, 111, 139
Record keeping, 36
Reinforcing, 147
Relationships
  art of old-fashioned, 3, 5
  building, in crisis, 35–39
  with customer, 165–66, 170, 171–72
  and defending against hostile takeover, 206–209
  and details, 136–37, 141, 145
  developing, 156
  and empathy, 74, 129
  and goal-sharing, 11
  and honesty, 34–35
  importance of, 133–45
  outside company, 37
  personalizing, 137–38
  and press, 149
  and selling, 95–99
  and success, 3, 4
  using other, 98–99
Reorganization, 35, 38
Resourcefulness, 4
Respect, 148

Restructuring, 20–21
Returning calls, 3
Robinson, Eddie, 10–11
Rogers, Kenny, 198
Rogers, Will, 159
Rogue tigers, 115–17, 120

Sacred cows, 18, 87–89
St. Andrews, Scotland, 140–41
Sales
  calls, 49
  closers, 37
  compensation, 106–20
  goals, 46
  and humor, 82
  and key symbol, 48
  and staying hungry, 219–21
  using "extended family" in, 99–101
Salespeople, 15, 16, 41–42
  and autonomy, 158–59
  and bankruptcy as selling point, 51–52
  and boundaries, 159–61
  and compensation, 106–20
  leader setting example for, 49–50
Sales support department, 109
Schembechler, Bo, 5
Schoolbus selling, 101
"Scrambling and winning" message, 56
Screen Paint, 212, 214
Secret or hidden assets, 95–99, 104
Seizing the day, 27–29
Selling
  company, 223–32
  by everyone in company, 99–101
  and humor, 81
  jungle, at the top, 90–105
  and Peachtree software, 195–97
  swarmselling, 101–3
  and *whatever it takes*, 60
Semper fidelis (fox), 93–94, 102, 104
Senior management, hiring, 77–78
Sensitivity, 114
Setbacks, 73
Severance pay, 34, 35
Sexual harassment, 117
Shareholders, 197, 204, 206–207, 208
Skruggs, Colonel, 94
Smith, Ed, 28
Smith, Howard, 41–42, 52
Software AG of North America, 142–43
software industry, 13–14, 155
Software products ventures
  early development of, 24–26, 31, 34
  feasibility of, 37–39
  and personal touch, 28–29
  and rights dispute, 61–62
  and "solving business problems," 56
Spangle, Clarence W. "Clancy," 205, 212–13
Speaking, public, 82–89, 89
Sports, 98
Stalking your goal, 3, 9–22, 29, 66, 211

Steinbrenner, George, 128
"Sterling silver person," 77
Stock
  and going public, 190, 191
  options, 207
  ownership, 118–19
  price, 14, 201, 204, 205
  repurchase, 207
Stockholder Systems, Inc., 61–62
Storytelling, 83
Stray cats, 128–29, 132
Success
  continuing, 210–22
  and control, 14–15
  and people, 4
Sudden strike, 23–26, 26–27
Super Bowl tickets, 56
Suppliers, 37
Survival of the desperate, 4
Survivors, 41–58
Swarmselling, 101–103, 105
SWAT team, 203, 205–207, 209
Swimming with the stream, 15
Switchboard operator, 14, 99
Symbols, 220
  importance of, 46–47
  and "Thanks to Banks" campaign,
    54–55
  using live, 173–79

Talker, 78
Tarkenton, Fran, 12–13, 15, 55–56, 100,
    131, 144–45, 150
Taxes, 2
  carryforward, 64–66
Teaching
  humor and, 81, 89
  vs. telling, 49–50
Team selling, 101
Technical development teams, 109
Technical evaluation, 50
Technical support, and *whatever it takes*,
    64. *See also* Customer service
Technology, 4–6, 127–28, 134–35
Teleconferences, 5
Telephone, 137–38, 207
Telling, vs. showing, 102
Temper, 126
Tenacity, 72, 75, 80, 228
"Thanks to Banks" theme, 54–55, 56
Themes, grand, 161–63
"Then that does, gets" rule, 106–20
Tiffany's, 47–48
Tiger(s)
  building den, 35–39, 40
  and company environment, 15
  compensating, 108
  defined, 1, 2–3, 3, 7, 234
  don't maul another, 111–13, 120
  family, and selling, 99, 104
  finding and hiring, 71–80
  key markers of, 72–74
  live, 162–63, 173–76, 177, 178–79

  motivating, in people, 6, 41–58
  never stop learning, 29
  origin of term, 173–74
  saving, 225–32, 234
  who doesn't own company, 11–12
Tiger's Club, 109
Time, not wasting, 99
Toffler, Alvin, 205
"Toos Disease," 17–18
Trade shows, 130
Trust Company of Georgia, 61
Trustee, 38, 62, 67
"Turnaround" theme, 220
Turnover rate, 76

U. S. Department of Justice, 25
U. S. Marines, 96
U. S. president, 73, 100–101
United Virgina Bankshares (UVB), 62–64,
    64
Univac, 94, 106–107, 154, 168
University Computing Company (UCC),
    19, 103–104, 130–31
Unnoticed, letting no one go, 114–15,
    120

Venture capital, 215
Versatility, 74, 80, 171
Vision, 45–46, 184–86
Visuals, 87
Vohs, Dennis, 64–65, 66, 128–29, 130–
    131
Voice mail, 5, 135

Walker, Tom, 57
Wall Street, 190–92, 212, 214, 215,
    216
Wall Street Journal, 52, 199
Wal-Mart, 12
Walt Disney Productions, 52
Walton, Sam, 12, 24, 149
Wang, Charles, 200–205, 206, 207
Wang, Tony, 208
Waterbed for bankers' convention, 39, 54,
    131
Watergate affair, 53
Watson, Tom, Jr., 92
Weiss, Warren, 49–50
Weissman, Bob, 226–27, 228, 229–
    230
Welke, Larry, 139–40
Wells, Brent, 59, 60, 124
Wendy's, 81
Whatever it takes, 59–67, 211
  and energy, 72
  and jungle clock, 64–66
  as operating phrase, 36, 50
  and pricing, 103
"What's In–What's Out" list, 88
Whitaker, Bebe, 45
W.H. Smith & Company, 172
Williams, Robin, 82
Wilson, Edmund, 106

Winners, 15
Winner's Circle, 109
Wounded, not leaving, 43–44, 50, 58
Wrestling, 96–97
Wyly, Sam, 19, 24

Yates, Charlie, 136
"You have to be a tiger to survive in '75" slogan, 174

Zachary's, 153–54
Zubay, Mary Ellen, 204–205, 205, 208